CW01044697

DUST

A True Story of a Naughty Beagle
Travelling Europe in a Motorhome

Emma and Ozwena Burton

Copyright © 2016 Emma Burton.

All rights reserved. No part of this book may be reproduced, stored, or transmitted by any means—whether auditory, graphic, mechanical, or electronic—without written permission of both publisher and author, except in the case of brief excerpts used in critical articles and reviews. Unauthorized reproduction of any part of this work is illegal and is punishable by law.

ISBN: 978-1-4834-4929-6 (sc)
ISBN: 978-1-4834-4928-9 (e)

Library of Congress Control Number: 2016905087

Because of the dynamic nature of the Internet, any web addresses or links contained in this book may have changed since publication and may no longer be valid. The views expressed in this work are solely those of the author and do not necessarily reflect the views of the publisher, and the publisher hereby disclaims any responsibility for them.

Any people depicted in stock imagery provided by Thinkstock are models, and such images are being used for illustrative purposes only. Certain stock imagery © Thinkstock.

Lulu Publishing Services rev. date: 4/21/2016

To Kath
Happy Travels
Happy Days
Emma Burton
X ♡

A True Story of a Naughty Beagle
Travelling Europe in a Motorhome

CONTENTS

Emma's Dedication:

This book is dedicated to my husband Paul, as without his inspiration, thoughtfulness, motivation and support this would never have happened. Paul is the most positive person I know and his good wit and loyalty have contributed to what I hope you find is a great read.

Paul is a one off, with a carefree attitude, a logical and stress free outlook on life and I can only strive to be more like him. My role model and the love of my life, he can spot the true value of a moment before it becomes a memory. Our determination pushes us forward to fill our lives with enjoyment and happiness and who knows what our next chapters will hold or where they will take us.

Maybe there is life after Dust!

Ozwena's Dedication:

In memory of my Miffy, our life together was cut far too short but once you allowed me into your space we bonded forever. Love always x

CHAPTER ONE

ABOUT ME - OZWENA BURTON

I am a Beagle known by the name of Ozwena. I was born on March 27th 2009 in a place called Birtley which is in the North East of England close to Newcastle upon Tyne. I lived in Birtley for a very short time with my brothers and sisters who rapidly disappeared every time there was a knock at the door.

This book is to put down into words my life so far. From Birtley to Wideopen in Newcastle, to a life on the road travelling through Europe in our Motorhome with my human parents, Paul and Emma and my adopted sister Uluru (Roo). I will go through all our experiences to date including the situations we (I) often find ourselves in and also tell you about the places we have visited A True Story of a Naughty Beagle Travelling Europe in a Motorhome.

The book comes from my perspective but as I'm sure you know, dogs cannot write or talk, even ones as clever as me, so Emma chips in and tells her side of the story too!

My life right now is amazing, especially the past eighteen months where I have travelled over 25,000 kilometres and visited over 19 different countries with my family.

You never know, my tail may even inspire you to travel, pack up your belongings, break free from the rat race and explore this beautiful world we live in. I can thoroughly recommend it.

Sit back and enjoy our story.

We used to live in a suburb of Newcastle, in a beautiful 1910 terraced house not too far away from the city centre. We had a large nature reserve close by which I visited and ran around numerous times every single day. I was familiar with every smell, and every nook and cranny where I would often find some form of food lying around. This space is, or rather was, my personal territory. My loud Beagle howl warned off any other four legged strangers that dared to step a paw there without my permission.

If I did see another dog that I didn't recognise I immediately raised my tail and heckles and raced towards them barking and howling until one of two things happened. They either turned and ran off in the opposite direction, or if they stood their ground, I would turn and run off in the other direction. I might pretend that I am tough, bossy and top dog but deep down I am just a coward, noisy and like my own way at times, well, all of the time really!

Obviously Roo was allowed in 'my space' in the nature reserve, as she is my sister, not my real sister of course as she looks nothing like me but she came into my life a few years ago and I will tell you more about her later on in my story. Back to the nature reserve I was telling you about and who I tolerate being there. Bailey and Bella are allowed, these are our oldest friends and are two spaniels, they smell pretty good and like to run just like I do. Others who have my permission to visit are my other friends Maisy and Mia and Hector. Roo's favourite friend is Hector as she flirts with him lots, she races towards him every time she sees him and she immediately lies on her back and he sniffs her from top to tail. She loves it!

Roo and I used to be walked by Paul and Emma around this park at least three times a day and although it was beautiful and ideal for dog walks we did sometimes get bored, though thankfully at weekends we would often go to different places. Visiting and exploring new territories is what I enjoy most of all as I get to sniff out different scents whilst Roo loves the beach, swimming in the sea and chasing her ball which she carries with her constantly.

I prefer the woods and forests and chasing rabbits and fox scents though I haven't yet caught any and to be honest I haven't thought about what would happen if I was to be successful. I find I am not as territorial in other places and tend to enjoy not having to warn off other dogs.

Despite the noise and first appearances I am quite a friendly and sociable dog. I love humans and meeting other four legged friends, sniffing their bottoms and letting them sniff my bottom in return. If I really like the smell of a particular dog I lie on my back and take pleasure in granting them access to smell my scent too. This is one of my favourite things in life. Meeting new friends and having my body sniffed and licked and I could lie there for hours and often do if the other dog is willing.

I am a fully bred Beagle and my official kennel club name is Harmony Birthday Girl, yet looking at me you wouldn't think I am a full pedigree. I don't look like a standard Beagle and often get told this by other people and my parents alike.

I was born with an elongated skinny frame, which now seems to be constantly expanding. I have a small head and large nose which everyone hoped I would grow into but haven't as yet! My fur is mostly black and I have a few blonde streaks down my back. My legs are white and very thin in comparison to my rather large and bloated stomach. It is now always bloated and is sometimes so tight and full of gas that it hurts. I can empty a room in seconds if I break wind and cannot control the toxic smells and this can happen in the most embarrassing of situations! My ears are large in comparison to my face and often get in the way of day to day tasks such as sprinting to the food bowl and they get wet when I drink from the water bowl. I am basically just a funny shape with only a few characteristics of a Beagle such as my loud howl and also the accustomed Beagle trait where I have the ability to disappear in the blink of an eye. Those of you reading this who know about us Beagles will know we cannot be trusted!

I am a female dog and know this is different to a boy dog as my brother had a dangly bit underneath him, whereas I've checked and I certainly don't have this. Strangely, although I'm a girl, I look like a boy and often get mistaken for a male. When we meet other people I hear them ask "how old is HE?" or "what is HIS name?" Paul always corrects them explaining that I am actually a bitch, which I always think is a bit harsh to call me this but he is my guardian and also my favourite person so I forgive him for this criticism!

I am a worrier and have always looked old, even as a puppy and the constant comments I hear are "yes he looks old" and "I cannot believe he is only six". Whilst I know I'm no oil painting I would like to point out that I feel that this isn't my fault.

Despite my idyllic lifestyle in my short years I have aged so much with all of the perceived stress, worry and anxiety I have to live with each day meaning that relaxing doesn't come easy to me.

In a way I kind of understand the boy comments as I presume it's easy and common to be mistaken for a boy. I do look very masculine and I don't help my cause by peeing like a boy with my hind leg cocked up at the back. This resonates from my puppy era and copying my brother, so now I don't know any other way to pee.

I have broad enough shoulders, literally, to accept these constant jibes about my appearance and have tolerated these for years now. I am just different, and being different is good right? "No one wants to be beige" Emma keeps telling me, "dare to be different" she says, which gives me the confidence I need.

There is nothing I can do about my appearance, apart from maybe having a Beagle face lift, or a Beagle nip and tuck. Though having visited some dog parlour establishments in the past and witnessed the procedure for certain pamper treatments I know that unfortunately I'm stuck with my odd features, crazy mind, moody personality and this is who I am.

Ozwena Burton formerly known as Harmony Birthday Girl. Ozwena Burton is the name on my pet passport though I usually get called Oz, Ozzie or he!

My name Ozwena is a little different to other names I hear and I don't know of anyone else called this. I do get called a number of variations from this such as Ween, Weenie, Bena, Been, Ozwena pickle, Oz, and Ozzie. I respond to all of these names …unless I am otherwise engaged in a more interesting activity such as eating, sleeping or rolling in poo. Emma invented this name for me using a variation of her favourite country Australia and also Wena meaning small warrior. Quite apt I think considering I was the runt of the litter.

Paul and Emma are my guardians now but I know they are not my real parents. My mother wasn't really interested in me and I didn't bond with her in the short time that I knew her. In her lifetime she'd had numerous pregnancies and had produced several other litters of Beagle puppies before me and this made her look old, tired, and very worn out.

He eyes were always glazed, her fur had no shine which troubled her, it was always falling out and it constantly itched her. She had eight very droopy boobies that would drag along the floor as she walked and they were in an awful state, all chewed and scarred from years of countless puppies pulling and nipping on them for milk.

I never really saw much of my real father either as he stayed outside in a kennel. I was never allowed to venture past the back door and I only got a glimpse of him as I was carried out of the house whilst Emma held me in her arms and he stared at me and looked upset. His eyes drooped and his ears sagged low, he had a nice face though and I can imagine he would have been a very handsome hound in his younger days. When I think back I always see his sad face and wished I had been able to know more about him.

Paul and Emma are lovely adoptive parents and I'm quite happy to stay with them as long as I can or however long they can tolerate me. Emma is nothing like my real mother for one she doesn't have droopy boobies and she is always happy but she can be annoying at times when she tries to kiss me which disturbs me especially when I'm sleeping.

Paul is my favourite though and I do adore him lots and I like to sit real close to him and rest my paw on his leg just to let him know I'm there. We have a strong bond that will never be broken.

Deep down I adore my family but I prefer to keep up a hard exterior and don't let this adulation manifest, in case they take me for granted. Reflecting on my behaviour I realise I do give them a hard time as I only allow cuddles and kisses on my terms which isn't very often and only when I can be bothered and in general these are reserved for Paul only. Emma and Roo rarely see my affection. I keep myself to myself in my own world which is often spent deep in thought or worrying.

Paul and Emma let me get away with most things, from jumping onto the sofa for a snooze, to pinching tasty treats from the table and making walks last twice as long as they should do, due to my disappearing acts. The bedroom in our house however was out of bounds. It always had been and now that it is five feet above the cabin in the motorhome it is a physical impossibility for me to even attempt the ascent.

I love to eat and my favourite food is tuna in oil, and as soon as the tin opens I am there sitting by Emma's side just waiting for a small flake to drop to the floor. I have a sixth sense where tuna is concerned and know what tin is being taken from the cupboard even before the tin is opened. This is a great skill I have and I could even hear this when sitting in other rooms in our house. Although hard to explain, I know by the sound of the tin if it has tuna in it and can differentiate the noise it makes when opened. I accept that unfortunately this skill probably won't take me anywhere in life but it is very useful at meal times and this is my favourite time of the day. The smell of the tuna once opened drives me wild and sends me into a spiral of madness until I get some. Tuna is a treat though and reserved for special occasions. Ninety nine times out of a hundred, mealtimes consist of dried biscuits and a spoonful of tinned meat which can get a little monotonous, hence the reason I scavenge at every opportunity.

I'm not a fussy eater at all and I do enjoy delicacies such as sheep, deer and horse poo! My favourite being sheep poo, delicious nuggets of doggy caviar just waiting to be feasted upon. Obviously I have these when out walking and off the lead, to my knowledge you can't get these in supermarkets, yet.

I'm more of a wolf it down eater than a connoisseur but I do find that all of the above have great flavour and texture and know I need to gobble these up as quickly as I can before I get caught. Whilst I focus mainly on sheep, deer and horse poo I'm not anti any animal or particularly fussy about what sort of poo it is. Emma does however go mad if she catches me eating this. She screams at me and gives me the command to "leave it". This leaves me with a dilemma to weigh up. Is the poo worth the telling off? My belly rules my head here and I think to myself 'no I will not leave it', to me this is a delicious treat, please leave me to enjoy this. I know that I do have selective hearing and pretend not to hear certain commands and furiously eat as much as I can before I invariably hear the clink of the lead being attached to my collar and get dragged away.

The only foods that I don't entertain are spinach, carrots and lettuce! They are no goes for this Beagle and I guess my eating habits stem from when I was a puppy having to fend for myself at the food bowl with my seven siblings, a mix of brothers and sisters who were always in my way and kicking and nudging me to the back of the queue.

Life as a puppy in Birtley was tough, I faced a constant struggle to get past my siblings to get to the food bowl. Attempt after attempt always led to failure and I would then have to wait at the back and eat any crumbs that had been left behind. Sometimes I didn't get anything at all and was left starving for hours until the next chance of a meal, where my struggles continued. My siblings were bullies as they used to nip and stand on me as they pushed past me, they used to keep me out of the way and they never allowed me to eat nor even have the chance to get some of the scraps were left over.

Thankfully, my meal times and the food situation gradually improved, as day by day our numbers decreased as the puppies left to go to their new homes. This made it easier for me to make my way to the food bowl but even after meal times I still felt the familiar pang of hunger. I never had the content feeling that I have nowadays of having a full and bloated stomach.

My determination in life stems from my upbringing when I was a puppy and the challenges I had when living with my siblings. Although nowadays I do suffer from anxiety, I have a strong mind and solid determination to achieve things in life such as escaping and running off to explore.

However, I am extremely loyal to my family especially Paul and have never given them any cause to be worried about me. Well that's my opinion anyway.

Another trait I have which other doggy parents will be able to relate to, is that I like to roll in poo and cover my full body from top to tail in the rich sweet scent of sheep, deer and fox poo. The smellier I can find the better with one of my favourites being when the strong scent of a rotten fish drew me towards it and I had great fun rolling and wriggling around on it like a break dancer. I smelt really good afterwards until I heard the familiar shrieks from Emma shouting for me to leave it! It's a great feeling to wriggle around in a dollop of poo to invigorate you, it gives you a real sense of energy, honestly if you've never done this before I recommend you try it!

Emma goes mad at me when I do this especially when she may not have noticed me doing this and once we get home she goes to cuddle me (unrequited) and then screams once she gets a whiff of me, resulting in her dragging me to the shower room to clean off all my hard work and beautiful scent. I do not like the shower or bath, in fact, I dislike water in general and only go in if I am forced and really have to. My howls and whimpering goes unnoticed and I complain until the awful event is over and I am again clean. Afterwards I like to be alone and find myself a quiet corner where I can sulk for a few hours until I snap out of it which usually happens strangely around my meal time.

CHAPTER TWO

MY FAVOURITE PERSON

My favourite person in the world and the whole universe is Paul, I am mad about him and he is definitely my best friend. I clearly remember the moment I first saw him. He came to visit me when I was just a small puppy and he stood in the kitchen and stared down at me and my brother as we were the only two left. He had long laces on his shoes and I pulled on these chewing them with my sharp teeth so that he would notice me. This didn't attract much attention so plan B came into play where I jumped up and down trying to make eye contact with him staring into his eyes as I was eager for him to pick me up.

Aside from me and my brother, all of our other siblings had been collected and had been taken to new homes. Although biased I have to admit my brother was adorable, he had a lovely glossy coat, huge brown eyes and he actually looked like a Beagle which I imagine is a good starting point if you are wanting to buy one.

Unfortunately I knew that I was not as adorable nor as cuddly as my brother so knew he could be a possible option, it was a fifty/fifty chance, me or him. I was the runt of the litter and I was weak and gasping for air when born and nearly didn't make it so haven't come out looking quite as adorable as him but I deserve a home and I willed him to pick me.

I could see Paul looking down at us both. I continued to squeal and jump up and down desperately hoping he would choose me and not my brother.

For days there had been knocks at the door, people appeared and one by one my siblings began to disappear. I was mentally willing myself to be chosen and kept a recurring thought that this has to be my time now. It was exhausting trying to be on our best behaviour all of the time as the constant trail of potential new owners visited each day to view us and decide which puppy they wanted to take.

My brothers and sisters used to tease me and leave me out of their play and food times. I never fitted in and was always just that bit different which they didn't like. Now there was just my brother and I left and he only tolerated me as there was no one left for him to play with. He would charge at me and nip and bite me to warn me off him and if I ever got too close he sometimes really hurt me.

I was sitting staring up at Paul and squealing to be picked up, but my yelps were largely ignored. I had noticed that he had brought another dog with him and another human called Emma. I watched the other dog and it certainly didn't want to be there. It was another Beagle, a female, a real pretty dog though it remained in the corner of the room and stood looking at the door waiting for it to be opened. It looked much older than me and looked angry to be there. I imagined it was a spoilt dog probably called princess, you and I both know the type. Just because they have been blessed with beauty they get away with so much more. One of my sisters was like that and she would put on her sad face and get away with pinching food and even peeing on the floor.

Eventually my yelps had the desired effect and Paul took notice of me and I felt the warmth of his hand pick me up and was lifted to his face that I simply stared at in delight. Come on "let's get out of here" I thought to myself as I willed him to take me to wherever he had come from.

He inspected me rather vigorously, lifting my ears and putting his fingers in my mouth to check my teeth, though aside from checking that they were real and not false I wasn't sure what he was looking for. I attempted to put what I would describe as my cutest face on and gazed at him in the hope he wouldn't put me back down. Emma was there too standing next to him and she too was gazing at me and she also inspected my fur, my paws and my teeth.

I was becoming overwhelmed by Paul's warmth as he held me and I felt a real connection and licked his nose and buried my head into his neck for warmth. He smelled amazing and I instantly fell in love. The distant yelps of my brother could barely be heard now and I was in my element being cooed over by Paul. The bond between us grew from that moment and he is still my master, my friend and my favourite person ever.

After a few words between the humans I sensed some positivity and guessed it was my time to leave as I was passed to Emma who also had a nice smell but not as nice as my hero Paul. This was my first hug from Emma and I licked her face which made her smile. She is alright I thought, but pass me back to Paul he is the one I want. Finding myself back on the floor with my brother I was confused as I thought they wanted me.

My first bit of good fortune in life didn't last long as a conversation indicated there was a problem with money. They hadn't brought any! The words ATM were branded back and forward and both Paul and Emma disappeared through the same door they had entered five long minutes ago. The dog which they had brought with them that was guarding the door didn't need to be asked twice and all three disappeared out the door and out of sight.

I was barely eight weeks old and this was definitely my lowest point. Lower than struggling to be born and lower than being ignored by my siblings.

The walls seemed to close in as I sulked back to my cage in the draughty, bleak and damp kitchen where we stayed and mid sulk I caught sight of my brother, looking at me with a smug look as if to say no one wants you and this is exactly what I was thinking. My whimpers sent me off into a deep sleep which was short lived my hopes raised again. I could hear the sound of voices and footsteps outside and another knock at the door. My eyes were all of a blur with the tears I had previously cried, yet they made out the images before me as being Paul and Emma, minus the pretty dog, and they were holding bundles of cash to buy me and take me to their home. I hoped they had sold pretty girl and used the money to buy me but deep down I knew this ATM person had given them the money.

As I sat upright in Emma's arms I watched as paperwork was completed and exchanged, then I was wrapped in a blanket and we left through the door, Oh yes! Harmony Birthday Girl was off to pastures new.

Despite our differences, before leaving I made an effort and wriggled free to see my brother and to say goodbye, he was hunched up in the cage where I had been only a few minutes ago, he looked sad his eyes filled with tears as I heard his whimper as we left. I felt sad leaving him and let out a yelp wishing he could come with us too and I do hope he found a nice family and he may even be as adventurous as me and also exploring the world, who knows.

As I was taken outside and up a small path out into the open air I realised I had never been out of the room before. It felt cold, the air was freezing, my hair stood up on end and I snuggled into the blanket trying to forget my brothers sad eyes which were the last thing I saw when leaving the house, my home and the only place I had known since being born. Outside was where my real father lived who I told you about earlier. This was the first and only time I saw him as I glanced back to see him in his cage, looking old and a little disheveled in much need for some love and comfort which I hope he found, but I very much doubt it.

I was trying hard to erase this sad feeling of leaving and the three of us got into a large metal object that bumped and swerved as it moved along. I was in the front with Emma on what I now know to be called the passenger seat. I heard a noise coming from the behind me and swivelled my head to find that the pretty and moody looking dog that they brought with them, the spoilt looking one, was there with us. She was a girl dog and both Paul and Emma made a lot of fuss of talking to her throughout the journey which she totally ignored. Pretty girl is what I called her, she looked feisty but I was sure she would be getting dropped off somewhere on the way to my new home.

This was all new to me and I had never been in the outside world nor been in any form of transport ever. Pretty girl looked furious that I had been chosen and even angrier that I was sitting on her favourite persons lap whilst she was locked behind bars in the boot. As we started to move my stomach churned and it was awful and I hated it! The moving sensation made me feel unwell but knew I had to make a good first impressions for my new family so fixated my eyes to the floor and settled into a state of meditation throughout the entire journey. I perfected this meditative state during this journey and this is something I still do on a regular basis. Maybe not daily but certainly on a weekly occurrence when I need to switch off.

To this day I still detest this vehicle and have linked this to a word I hear often being called a car! I shudder every time I hear this word and cry and whimper so I don't have to go into it.

You're probably thinking how does a dog that gets travel sick on a short journey manage to circumnavigate Europe and that would be a fair question. Simple answer is the motorhome we have seems to agree with me. Whether it is the extra space or slower speeds I actually enjoy travelling in it. I'm sure at some stage I'll have to put this to the test and start travelling again by car, but that's something I cannot think about right now.

Emma has tried to help me with my fear of the car and has given me medicine before we had to go anywhere but this for me, was an even worse experience than going in the car itself. I do not like to take any medication and like my sixth sense with the tin of tuna being opened I can hear the tablets being taken from the box and then know what's coming. When I hear this cracking noise I instantly clamp my jaws together and lock them so that nothing can enter my mouth. Emma struggles to try and open my mouth but never succeeds. Nothing can get into my mouth and I clench my teeth together as tightly as I can. She tries to fool me by hiding medication in sausages and pate but I know what's in them as I can smell it. All I do is simply lick the delicious meat from the tablet and then spit it out. To this day I will not take a tablet or medicine, ever!

I'm a clever hound and recognise and understand lots of words that humans say, in various languages I may add. Paul and Emma often talk to me and I understand the words breakfast, tea, food, walk, run, treats, biscuits and cuddles, and of course my favourite word of all, Paul. I think Emma likes to wind me up by saying "where is Paul?" and no matter where I am or what I am doing, I strain my eyes to see where he is. Sometimes I sit at the windows for ages just looking to see where he is and waiting for his return.

Back in the car and I am still in a deep form of meditation, the journey lasted for what seemed like ages and I sat in Emma's arms meditating not making a noise the entire way, I was on my best behaviour. She cuddled me which made me feel happier as I had never really been cuddled before but more importantly I just wanted this awful moving sensation to stop!

Pretty girl was still sitting in silence behind me and hadn't really made any eye contact with me. I was puzzled and wondered who she was and if she would be staying with us and if so, for how long.

Eventually the motion of the car stopped and my anxiety and nausea instantly stopped. I peeked through the gap in the blanket that I was still wrapped in to take a look outside. I saw a large house with a garden. This must be my new home and it looked nice, there was grass and trees and I felt excited to get out and give this place a good sniff.

Paul got out of the car and opened the back door where pretty girl jumped out. I watched as she barged her way through the black metal gate and into the garden. She moved up the pathway and then waited at the front door for it to be opened. A black door with brass numbers on it. Pretty girl was a large dog, quite plump if I do say so myself, she looked grumpy and was clearly older than me but I was still wondering who she was.

Emma took a while longer to reach the gate with me still in her arms as she walked slowly, holding me gently. However, I wanted out and I wasn't bothered about warmth and wriggled free jumping from her arms and raced through the front door where I was met by a fierce looking pretty girl. Skirting past her and not wanting to invade her privacy just yet by giving her a sniff I continued with my exploration of the house sniffing every nook and cranny.

We were all now inside the house and seeing pretty girl in her fur lined dog basket in the living room made the penny drop. I guessed that this dog lives here too and approached her gingerly and eagerly to sniff her out and offer a paw of friendship.

She still wasn't making any eye contact so I pushed my nose towards her and tried to get a good sniff of her but as I went in for a smell she turned around and snapped at me. Whoa! I was slightly shocked yet for some reason was not frightened by her so I just thought it best to give her leave her for the rest of the day especially when food was around as she was definitely the top dog in this house. I knew this by the way Paul and Emma treated her. The way she would be wrapped in a fur blanket, lifted up and cuddled, and when she liked to stretch out on the comfy sofa, they allowed it meaning they sometimes had to sit on the floor. This was very different to where I had just come from and it was going to take some getting used to. I instantly knew my place and pretty girl was more than happy to remind me of this to make sure I was always in her shadow. I followed her from a distance as with me being so much smaller at the time I was cautious in case she hurt or tread on me, accidentally or on purpose, so always made sure I kept my wits about me, again another trait I learnt from my time with my siblings.

This was to be my first night in my new home and I felt so excited to be with my new parents and also with my new sister who I was sure would warm to me soon, I couldn't wait. Just then I heard the telephone ring and heard Emma talking to someone about me. "Oh we can't make it as we just bought a new puppy" she said. Ah that is me I thought. She continued. "It's not fair on her first night, I couldn't leave her." I was straining my ears to hear all of the conversation. "No no" she said "we better not", then "oh really ah go on then what time will we meet?" My ears fell to the floor in bitter disappointment. You can't go out it's my first night in my new home and I stared at Emma in disbelief!

The conversation ended with ok *"I'm sure Alex will love to have her for the night"*. What! Who is Alex? Does she definitely mean me and am I going to Alex's house? This cannot be right. What about my new home, my new family and bonding time with my new sister.

Oh no this is not a good start….Sure enough fifteen minutes later a knock at the door and in came Alex. She was beautiful and she smelled really good. I ran towards her as fast as I could and jumped up at her willing her to pick me up. She cupped me in her arms and hugged me tightly. I liked this Alex person and I felt safe with her so off she took me for the night where I stayed at her home.

Her house was huge and way bigger than the one I had just left. I was greeted at her front door by her two very friendly spaniels Bailey and Bella who are now two of my closest friends, I told you about them earlier who I used to play with at our nature park.

Bailey the eldest of the two and the princess and ruler of the household. What Bailey wants to do, she will do. Bella is more relaxed and laid back and I soon settled in and Bella let me share her bed for the night.

Alex was a kind person and after a very pleasant night I would happily have stayed with her for a little longer but a knock at her door the next morning saw Paul and Emma return and I just melted when I saw Paul again and the feelings of love for him came over me. Take me home I pleaded. I gave out licks of affection for my overnight sleep companions and left, happy knowing I was welcome back at any time.

After that, Bailey and Bella would often call around to our house and we used to have great fun chasing one another around the house racing up and down the stairs and making an all mighty racket. One Sunday evening when they called to see us, they had just been out for a very long walk and were exhausted. We were all settled and happily snoozing when this awful smell started to seep through the walls, the floor boards and the draft from under the door.

Urghhh what is that smell? It was so strong it woke me up but Bailey and Bella were still both snoozing beside me. Emma could smell this too and pushed open the living room door to investigate and was greeted by two huge mounds of doggy poo. Enormous size mounds at that. Had an elephant made its way into our house whilst we were sleeping or had Bailey and Bella mistakenly deposited two massive piles of brown poo in our hallway? Emma rushed to get the cleaning fluid and cleared them up and washed the floor until it was spotless and I noted she had to use several bags to collect the poo. Personally I was shocked and couldn't believe they waited to poo here in our house and not outside on their walk. Even at eight weeks old I knew if I had done that I would have been scolded.

During the first few days living in my new home I would occasionally try to take a peek of pretty girl, who obviously didn't want to know me. Even looking at her seemed to annoy her and she growled and snapped at me whenever I got close and tried to make friends with her.

This happened for the next few weeks and I just accepted that this was how it was to be and with that acceptance our relationship started. Gradually, with time she warmed to me and although I knew I was never going to be the top dog and would remain forever in her shadow, I grew to love her a lot, even though the feeling wasn't mutual as she only ever mildly tolerated me being there.

She continued to warn me on several occasions that it was her house and I had to abide by her rules. She communicated this in a firm way as she towered over me physically, stamping her authority that I was merely an acquaintance, to not make eye contact nor look at her unless it was on her terms.

Myfanwy (Miffy) was our beautiful Beagle who Paul and I adored. She was eighteen months older than Ozzie and despite being non pedigree she was the perfect Beagle in every way. We bought Ozzie for her with the idea being that they would be good together, to keep each other company as they are pack animals. However this thinking and their bonding relationship didn't quite start the way we had wanted it to.

No doubt about it Miffy was top dog of the house and was very spoilt and set in her ways. She had a lovely soft nature about her which made her even more adorable than she already was. We had taken her along to see Ozzie when we collected her as a puppy thinking it would help with the bonding process and that she would be overjoyed to have a sister to look after. She did after all have plenty of friends on her daily walks whom she loved and we reasoned the company would do her the world of good on the rare occasions she was left alone.

Miffy enjoyed having people around her and was in her element if we had a house full of friends. She carried a Santa hat everywhere with her and would go mad if I took it away to wash as it used to get quite smelly. She wouldn't settle until she had it back. They say a dog isn't just for Xmas, well in this case neither was the santa hat! This hat was her best friend and she carried it everywhere holding the pom pom bit in her mouth. She was protective over this and didn't like anyone else moving or touching it.

When she slept she used to lie with it in between her legs so the pom pom bit tickled her stomach and sometimes she would do a humping action with it furiously releasing all of her frustration then lie in a trance for a while afterwards and then repeat this time and time again until she was exhausted and eventually went to sleep.

Ozzie used to watch her transfixed with a puzzled look trying to work out what on earth she was doing. This was both embarrassing and also entertaining when we had friends to visit as Miffy liked to show everyone what she could do. In she would stroll, Santa hat in mouth, taking centre stage in the middle of the living room floor to show us her party trick.

My big sister did eventually start to mellow a little as the days and weeks passed and it wasn't until one day when I was sleeping in my bed that I felt her climb in and cuddle in next to me and that day I knew I had finally been accepted and this was now my home. At this breakthrough moment I didn't want to move even though she was a lot bigger than me and was crushing my head with her large paws. I was just happy and relieved that she had come to be with me and this made me happy. I remember lying as still as can be with her heavy weight on me making it difficult to breathe and move but I was content that she had finally accepted me in her house.

Miffy would however remind me that she was always the boss and gave me gentle reminders of this when I over pawed the mark. Such as if I moved in the wrong way or tried to have a lick of her food bowl after our meal times.

I grew to like the authority she had as I knew where I stood with her. I always allowed her to walk in front of me on walks and she was always front of the queue for any treats or cuddles that we would often get.

Miffy was unbelievably attractive for a dog, her fur was soft and her nose had huge red freckles, her ears were velvety soft and when we went out walking we would often get stopped by people who cooed over her admiring her beauty. Whilst this happened I stood next to her, obviously invisible and as usual going completely unnoticed.

I followed her everywhere much to her disgust! I watched how she interacted with other dogs and how she used to chase and pick up scents when we were out on our walks.

I was her shadow and when she jumped through our dog flap in the door for the toilet then so did I. She taught me everything that I know today including the good things like knowing how to use the toilet outside and also the bad things such as when I run away on walks and ignore the calls and whistles to go back!

Miffy and I had great fun running and chasing rabbits and following deer scents as we ran through the long grass that tickled our stomachs as we raced for hours having a great time. One day we ran away for miles and miles and ran for hours until it turned dark, we realised we were hungry and didn't know which way was home and we panicked. It was a cold night and the ground was wet and icy, we both felt exhausted and we were desperate for some water and food.

We had such a great time before stopping running and realising that we were very lost and wanted to be home. After an age we were relieved to finally hear the familiar sound of Emma whistling in the distance. We had both been howling in the hope that somebody would hear us but no one had showed up to get us. We heard her calls and whistles and we headed back in that direction and were eventually reunited with her.

We never did learn our lesson however, as most walks we went on always saw us take the opportunity to run away and chase the scents of various animals. We used to run away for hours and sometimes lost track of time and headed back home once it had turned dark. We always got wrong but the consequences of being scolded were worth it and we could cope with the silent treatment for a while.

It didn't matter as Miffy was always very soon forgiven, which in turn meant I was too and then in time we were allowed to jump up onto the sofa as if nothing had happened, with cuddles and treats for us both.

My bond with Miffy grew stronger and stronger every day and although I knew she didn't care if I was there or not I really loved her. She was unpredictable, sometimes she would warm to me and allowed me to sit with her on the sofa and even sleep in the same bed as her but other times she made it clear she wanted her own space which left me alone in my bed all night.

Miffy was a greedy dog, even greedier than me and that's saying something. She once ate a handbag which had been left on the living room floor after a party at our house. It had been left downstairs when everyone had gone to bed at night and Miffy could smell that it had something sweet inside.

I watched cautiously from a distance as Miffy opened the bag scratching it with her paws and ate the full contents, lipsticks, handkerchiefs, some gloves, oh and not forgetting the tube of mints which had first tempted her.

She continued devouring the whole handbag only leaving the hard metal bits that she just couldn't stomach. Just like that, bag ate and gone.

I had been tempted to have a go but she warned me to back off on several occasions so I just left her to it and personally I prefer food not bags! Later that night the house was quiet and felt cold so we both wandered upstairs and wriggled in between the two humans that were staying in our spare bedroom. We didn't know them that well and I'm sure they didn't mind us being there after all they were Paul and Emma's friends so now they were our friends too. It was nice and warm there and the humans didn't stir at all so we slept soundly through the night.

It was early in the morning when I was woken to hear the sound of Miffy being sick. The gurgling sound and retching she made, also woke the humans, just in time for Miffy to display her grand finale of spewing vomit all over the mattress and bed sheets where she had been sleeping.

I can still remember the noise of the shrieks and screams coming from the bedroom that morning. Emma had the job of cleaning up the mess and the vomit she had brought up containing what looked like the contents she had eaten from the handbag. The apologies Emma made to our guests were never ending that day. Come to think of it, they never did stay at our house again.

There was another time when there was a few people at our house as Paul and Emma often had parties which meant Miffy and I would end up being fussed over, fed lots and then ignored. One of the people at this party didn't seem to like us and every time we walked into the room she would jump and scream "get them out!" Miffy and I were then shooed out into the other room and furious about this as there was a serious amount of food going on in there.

At night as they all slept Miffy and we crept up the stairs and into the bedroom, where Miffy curled into a tight ball on top of the persons head, quite predictably it was the one who didn't like us much. I think some alcohol had been consumed as the person who was fast asleep didn't move or respond until she woke in the morning and again I can still recall the shrieks and screams that came from the bedroom that morning.

CHAPTER THREE

MY MIFFY

I've never been ill and aside from an operation that would prevent me from becoming a mother to my own puppies I'm proud to say that I've never had to visit a vet for an illness. I did once have a splinter in my paw which caused some slight discomfort and my right hind leg and paw now swell up after particularly long walks but apart from that I have always been lucky and kept myself in good health. My nose is shiny and black and always has a nice wetness about it which I am told, is a healthy sign.

On the other paw my sister Miffy was never away from the vet and we would all have to go to the surgery, sometimes once, sometimes even twice a week. Despite being in impeccable health I would have to go along with them for the journey and ride in the boot of the car which I hated as the motion of the car moving unfailingly still made me feel nauseous but as these were such relatively short journeys I learned to cope in my meditative state. I was used to the routine now and as soon as we arrived and entered the surgery Miffy would get taken away and I would just sit and wait in a cold and soulless waiting room that quite frankly smelt awful. I detested our visits there and it always felt like I was there for hours. Sitting waiting for Miffy to return after having whatever treatment or check-up was scheduled for her.

This had been the routine for some time now and I figured that these visits meant that Miffy was not very well and she also smelled differently and slept for longer and more often. I tried to be supportive by giving her cuddles when she was sleeping to make her feel loved and to keep her warm and for once she didn't seem to mind my invasion. The alarm bells started ringing when she began to leave her food which was not like her at all! Like the good dog and sister I am I helped her out with this and ate this for her. Emma used to make her some very tasty foods to try and entice her to eat and as I watched this food being created and put down in front of her I couldn't understand why she wouldn't eat this, it was delicious and far nicer that the stuff we were used to getting.

After months of living with this routine it reached the point where Emma had to take her further afield to a specialist hospital that meant we had to get into the blasted car again where we drove for miles, up past the Northumberland coast, into a new country and a place called Edinburgh. I was now an expert in the art of meditation and put this to the test with my longest meditation to date. All of the way there and all of the way back in one day. For me this was a long distance, four hours in total, and my job when we were at our destination was to stay in the awful smelling waiting room until Miffy had seen by the vet.

We had to endure this journey several times and every time we left I knew Miffy was becoming weaker. Her illness and the length of the journey allowed us to move from the boot of the car and onto the back seat where she was laid down so she could stretch out her full body.

My world fell apart when my beloved sister Miffy died of something called cancer in February 2010. It was a miserable dark, cold and grey afternoon and she was taken away from me, from us all.

I do miss Miffy so much and losing her means I now suffer from anxiety and have nightmares when I think about her which makes me so sad and triggers even more panic and anxiety. Miffy and I had some great times together but sadly for reasons I do not understand she is gone, forever. I knew she was ill but thought she would get better and stay with me but somehow one day she was there and the next she was gone.

I remember it vividly. It was a Monday lunchtime, a young man came into the house, I recall voices and then heard crying. I scratched at the living room door for it to be opened to see what was happening and then it opened and Miffy was carried past me, followed by Paul and Emma, into the back yard, wrapped in a blanket and taken away in our car and that was the last time I saw her.

I was left alone, confused, afraid in my empty and silent home, no Emma, no Paul and no Miffy anymore. The house felt so empty without Miffy and I was missing her really badly and spent the next couple of hours looking out of the window for her to come back. "Come on Miffy where are you?" My mind playing tricks as a few times I thought I saw her running in through the front gate and into the house and I raced downstairs for the door to open but it never did. I wished she would come back, I howled, cried and pined for her return.

After a long wait Paul and Emma came back home with no Miffy and I went wild when I saw them. I couldn't control my panic, my screams and my crying and I just wanted to be cuddled and close to them. They too were crying and knew something dreadful had happened as they never cry and this sent me into a deeper state of anxiety. Emma tried to comfort me by giving me some medicine that she believed would calm me down, by sneaking it into a piece of meat which she knows I won't take, I couldn't think, never mind eat.

I never settled that day and for weeks after couldn't sleep or eat nor function without her being there with me. I hated being alone and not having Miffy with me and I continued to cry just wishing she would come back and live with us again.

Since Miffy left us I continued with this awful feeling that something was missing and my anxiety stayed with me for some time and I still carry this with me even now every day. The knots in my stomach and the constant pang of emptiness and anxiety I feel is now part of me and I guess will never fully go away. Sometimes I have good days and also bad days when all these memories come flooding back.

I heard a person telling Emma that she was only a dog! Grrrrrr she was my best friend and people who don't like us dogs just don't understand. Miffy brought me some great times, a lifetime of memories and great entertainment. She was well known locally and when we were all strong enough to we ventured out of the house for walks, just the three of us and people would stop and ask us where she was.

She was a real show stopper, a beautiful dog and it is little comfort that the short time we spent together was so enjoyable. She leaves us with sadness in our hearts that she was taken from us too soon. She was barely three years old, which is far too young but I try and console myself in the fact that the life she had with us couldn't have been any better.

Following this episode I developed separation anxiety and the routine went something like this. If Paul and Emma went out they usually left through the front door. I immediately jumped into the back yard through the dog flap and would remain motionless in the yard until they returned. This was done regardless of the weather so I would often be soaked to the skin when they returned where I would jump back through the dog flap into the kitchen to run and greet them. My condition became so bad that I was taken to a doggy shrink for some counselling. I was examined and observed and given some tablets, which I refused to take so this didn't really help the situation either. I did receive extra cuddles and kisses which sometimes made me feel happier though other times I found it easier to drift into my own world, in my meditative state of calm.

Ozzie has never been the same since Miffy died and her depression and anxiety has aged her quite considerably. To the extent that she looks much older than her six years. She has saggy eyes and a constant facial expression which screams worry and fear, a bit like the expression you get from a rabbit when they are confronted by car headlights.

Both Paul and I tried to help her by taking her to a therapist, giving her more cuddles, quality time out for walks and socialising with her doggy friends but losing Miffy changed her outlook and she was no longer a fully content and happy dog.

We too were suffering the loss of Miffy as she was such a big part of our lives. Our first dog had gone and whilst we knew that dogs don't last forever we were expecting more than three years with her. The cancer she had was an aggressive form in her lymph glands and the chemotherapy treatment she had was carried out in the Edinburgh vetinary specialist hospital who cared for dogs with this type of cancer. This meant long drives, travelling to and from Edinburgh which took up our weekends and evenings, our focus being to get her to the hospital for her appointments and treatment and caring for her when she was sick.

Paul and I were devastated after the diagnosis of Miffy's cancer which was found and diagnosed only a few months before her death. She was in real pain and discomfort and as soon as her last zap of chemotherapy was given to her the vets confirmed that they could do no more and that was the end of the road for our favourite girl.

We adored and spoilt her and she repaid us with unconditional love and gave many hours of fun and happiness. Every day she showered us in kisses and never showed favouritism between Paul and I which made me love her all the more. She was top dog in our house and we would often find ourselves sitting on the floor just so Miffy could lie and stretch out on the sofa. We really missed her and still do and all we have left of her now are photographs, and we have an annual tribute where we light a candle for her on her birthday.

We were lucky to have each other for support as we continued to grieve and this pain of loss stayed with us for weeks but for poor Ozzie it was worse and her anxiety took hold of her in a manner that completely turned her life upside down. To counter and prevent the bizarre ritual of her standing outside alone in the back yard whenever we left the house we arranged for dog sitters to be with her and Paul would work from home on occasions to keep her company but we both knew that this couldn't continue as financially this was a real expense and we also didn't want to continue living with a depressed dog. Something had to be done!

CHAPTER FOUR

ULURU

I was sitting on my favourite seat in the front room just where the chink of sun comes through the window. It was nice and warm and I drifted off into a hazy snooze. My anxiety doesn't allow me to sleep soundly and at times still torments me. I could hear Emma talking in the other room and then I heard my name being called. For once I decided to respond to a command and went to find her where I was greeted with the familiar clink sound of my lead being attached to my collar. "Oh no, don't take me out". I really wasn't in the mood.

We walked out of the house, out of the front garden and in the direction of Maisy and Mia's house. As we followed the pavement, I could smell them which confirmed we were getting closer and were going to see them. My mood lightened as I loved going to their house, I got really spoiled there. For example, feeding time consists of cooked chicken, mince, steaks and anything else that most other dogs don't usually get. Not the same bowl of dried disappointment that gets rolled out for my meal times.

Miffy and I used to stay with them occasionally before we got banned for a while after Miffy fell into the pond and ate one of the fish by mistake! She actually did the same when we went to another friend's house. Splash, in she fell, fish gobbled up and funnily enough we were never invited back there either.

Maisy and Mia greeted me at their front door and we raced around the garden, with one dodging around me and the other knocking me in a semi friendly way to remind me this was their territory and not mine.

Maisy is a young black dog with a beautiful face, she smells like me and we have a good bond. Mia is a couple of years older than me, a tall slender larger dog, she keeps me in line and always prevents me from getting to the food bowl first. She gets more cuddles from her owner than any dog I've ever met and whilst she can be quite dominant with me and all of her possessions I don't mind as I have Maisy to play with.

After running in the garden for what seemed like hours I noticed my anxiety had dipped a little and realised that I hadn't thought about Miffy as much that afternoon which then started to make me feel guilty and lo and behold my anxiety started. Emma had also disappeared from view and I guessed she escaped whilst I had been outside chasing Maisy.

It was getting late and as well as being hungry I was worrying about where Emma had got to and if she would ever come and collect me. Is this my home now? It's nice I like it here but I wanted to go home. I sat at the front window, downstairs, as they don't have an upstairs for some reason, looking and waiting for Emma to arrive. I sat rigid like a statue at the window, my stomach starting to grumble with hunger, the delicious foods around me were not appealing as I was feeling anxious and worried now and stayed transfixed and motionless at the window.

Eventually I saw the familiar sight of the dreaded car which for the record I still detest. I jumped from the chair that I had been perched on for hours waiting for this moment and raced to the door. I could hear and smell Paul and Emma and I pushed my nose tightly under the door so I could smell more.

A loud knock at the door followed and this sent me hysterical it was definitely them. My barking and whining was deafening and I howled with delight as the door was opened. I missed them and I jumped up and howled as I was so happy they had come back for me.

I remember seeing Emma first and that she was holding something in her arms. I looked closer and saw she had a fluffy ball of blonde fur in her arms. Oh no, it better not be a cat, I thought. She hasn't went and bought a cat has she? I don't like cats! I jumped up and strained to see what it was. First of all I saw a black glossy nose, huge brown eyes that were looking straight at me. Oh thank goodness it wasn't a cat. I squealed with excitement as Emma unfolded the blanket to reveal the most adorable puppy and I gave her a sniff which confirmed she was a girl the same as me, hooray!

Gradually she unraveled herself from the blanket she was wrapped in and placed on the floor in front of us, all eyes were fixed on her. She had bright strawberry blonde fur, extra-long skinny legs and amazing dark brown glossy eyes. She glanced up at me and as soon as our eyes met we went into a frenzy of madness racing around the garden chasing each other. Even though she was the smallest, tiniest thing I had ever seen she was fast and I was so happy to have a new play mate. For the first time in months my tail was high in the air and I pranced walking high on my toes showing off that I was a proud hound with responsibilities now, I had a brand new sister to look after.

When all four of us arrived at our home, the front door was left open and all of our friends and family came to see the new addition to the household. I remembered my first day in my home was faced with challenges I had with Miffy and then being taken to Alex's house at night, the warm welcome that my new sister got here was quite different.

I watched as a continuous stream of people entered the house, ignored me and simply cooed over this small ball of fur all commenting on how adorable she was. What is it about puppies that make people go all weird, and gushy, they even speak differently? "Oh isn't she a cutey wooty?" it doesn't make sense and as usual nobody at all acknowledged me. The new puppy was getting all of the attention and I quickly realised that I'd be living in her shadow, just as I did with Miffy.

I also realised after only a few days of having her in my life that my new sister was a crazy girl, full of energy and she got away with a lot more than

I did at her age. Even when she squatted and had a pee on the floor in the house, she didn't get shouted at.

She didn't yet know that dogs have to go outside to use the toilet and I knew that I'd have to teach her, just as Miffy had taught me only a few years ago. I showed her the door to use, how to open the flap to get outside and where to pee. Uluru was her name and yes she was naughty, she tried to steal my food, toys and chewed my favourite chair, ripping this to bits which meant I could no longer sit on it. Despite this I loved her attitude and fun outlook in life which made me love her more and more each day.

As a puppy she liked to play fight and had so much energy which kept me busy and exhausted for days on end. She soon tired though and we did get some rest where she would just collapse and fall asleep for a while until she'd wake with a start and be refuelled with more energy to burn off.

I was exhausted but thankful for the chaos she brought into my life. Most of all she filled a void and filled my heart with the fun and energy that I hadn't felt for a long time since losing my Miffy.

Paul and I had decided that Ozzie needed some company and had spent evenings looking on the internet for breeds of dogs and litters that were soon to be available. Our decision to get another dog was the only option we had left after trying all of the other options suggested to us when living with a grief stricken anxious dog. Our search was soon narrowed down to two breeds. Weimaraners and Fox Red Labradors. Both similar sized and good breeds for running with us and enjoying long walks.

We found a Fox Red Labrador available at a farm in Wakefield. Around a two hour drive for us. We asked the owner to send some pictures and the first one she sent through melted our heart. It came with the caption, "this is my foxy lady" and she looked absolutely perfect. Decision made, she was ready to collect and we made arrangements to drive down and collect her the following weekend.

Aside from getting lost on route and knocking on the wrong door which by chance was a Spaniel breeder, we arrived at the correct location and collected her with the minimum of fuss. As it was a four hour round trip we had left Ozzie with friends and had remembered to take money this time for the purchase of our new puppy.

Seeing the foxy lady in real life melted our hearts, she was perfect and even more beautiful in the fur than in the photograph the breeder had sent us. We watched as she made her way to the doorway of the pen where her and all of the other puppies were happily playing with one another. I reached over the small fence and picked her up and she wrapped herself around my neck where she stayed for the remainder of our journey back to Newcastle and to this day she hasn't stopped cuddling me.

We decided to call our new arrival Uluru or Roo for short, due to the beautiful bright red coat she has, which reminded us of Ayers Rock in Australia which we visited when we spent time travelling a good few years ago. Uluru is the aboriginal name for Ayers Rock and when we visited this monument, the colour of the rock was a deep red colour when the sun shines on it, just the same as our Roo.

We were happy and relieved that Ozzie quickly accepted Roo into her home and thankfully we were so pleased that Ozzie seemed happier, now that she had a puppy disturbing her sleep and her routine. Roo would jump on her, bite her ears and nip her ankles. Ozzie never became irritated and just allowed it to happen and she gradually started to show signs of contentment sleeping more and wagging her tail more often. Her regular trait of standing outside when we left the house also stopped which made us realise that buying Roo was the best thing we had done for her. To this day Ozzie still does have highs and lows and often dips into a depression and doesn't have the same sparkle in her eyes and whilst we are fully unsure as to why she gets like this, maybe a throwback or memory of Miffy, thankfully nowadays her down days are few and far between.

I was overjoyed to find that my anxiety subsided whenever Paul and Emma left Roo and I alone in the house. No more jumping out of the dog flap to stand like a statue in the back yard. I knew Uluru needed me and my new role to be her sister and provide her with company made me feel like I had a purpose in my life. Roo and I would snooze together sleeping in our bed, wrapped up and tangled in each other's paws. We snoozed for hours and I quickly got used to feeling Roo's warm belly next to me.

I know that Roo is Emma's favourite and I notice this especially at meal times when I see Emma Shovelling food into Roo's bowl and her portions getting bigger and bigger whereas mine are still a small portion of the same old dried dog biscuits. I used to try and eat mine quickly so I could get some of Roo's but she eats quicker than me devouring her extra-large portion which disappears in seconds.

Roo always gets the best chews from the packs of goodies that used to be kept in the food cupboard which we often observed. For Roo, food is life, and is one of the most important things for her apart from Emma. Like Miffy she is a greedy dog and she soon realised where the best cupboard in the house was and where the food came from.

Like me she loves being outside, walking, running and chasing her ball but nothing compares with the feeling she gets when she knows it is time to be fed. When left alone in the house we would hunt like a small pack, sniffing every inch around the food cupboard in the hope that a tasty snack or even a crumb had fallen out. We spent a lot of time inspecting this area and gave it an organised check over several times throughout the day. One day to our delight we noticed it had been left open and Roo broke her way in and devoured the full bag of food leaving only a few stray biscuits for me. Emma caught us in action and her shrieks were so loud we dashed out through the dog flap. Whilst I managed the escape, Roo's bulging stomach prevented her from being able to get out and after consuming what was the equivalent of a week's worth of food, she wasn't going anywhere. Of course she was punished with cuddles and soon forgiven! Grrrrrrr

Without fail Roo gets far more cuddles in the house than me and always more cuddles and attention from the other humans that we meet. Just like Miffy did when she was around. Roo now gets all the compliments and cuddles from people who say "isn't she beautiful" "isn't she gorgeous" familiar phrases that I often hear but sadly ones that are never directed at me.

I don't mind this really as I quite like being in the background but it would be nice to occasionally get some recognition of actually existing. Like I say I'm used to this now as everyone we meet instantly adores Roo and then if I'm very lucky will get a nod of the head in my direction often followed by the comment "what sort of dog is that?" or the old favourite, "what's his name?"

CHAPTER FIVE

DUST

Roo fills me with such joy and happiness but I do still miss Miffy and think of her most days though not every day now as Roo keeps me occupied and busy. When Miffy died she was taken to a doggy crematorium and on her return appeared in a completely different form from the one she had left us in. Her large frame of 19kg and all of her beauty appeared in a very small wooden box. Amazingly, I now know that this is her remains, everything and all of her packed densely inside. A dark brown box with her name on a brass plate and inside there is heavy thick grains of dust that show no resemblance of her what so ever.

This box of dust doesn't misbehave like she used to nor does it steal and eat my food. I poked my head into the small hole of the box to sniff this dust and doing this I'm happy that she is back with us. Yes I admit it's in a completely different form but as long as she is here then I want the box to stay. In the evenings I used to like the box close to me and Emma would place this next to me in my bed as I slept.

Emma had collected her ashes from the crematorium and sat with me to explain that when Miffy died she was cremated and the dust in the box, well, that was her remains.

I sat very still and concentrated whilst she spoke but this was way too complicated for me to understand and to this day I still occasionally try to fathom this out. I look at the box, sniff it and have to admit that yes it does smell like her but it certainly doesn't look like her at all!

At first I expected Miffy to jump out of this and surprise me, but this never happened. When I first took a closer look inside I gave this dust a sniff and instantly knew it was her in there. All of those familiar smells and memories from the previous two years came back to me.

The weeks following her death saw my mind race with constant thoughts of Miffy, about her death, the dust in the box and the crematorium thing that Emma explained. As you can imagine this was a lot of information for a small Beagle brain like mine to take in though I think I've worked it out and I'm right in thinking that, you live, you get ill, you die, and then you turn to dust!

Because of this awful experience I am so thankful that I have a family that has taken me with them to travel in our motorhome through Europe. This is what I needed to do with my life and I want to keep on exploring and living and learning about all the places, walks, continental foods, both bought and foraged and new smells all around the world and hopefully we will keep on going.

Most of my doggy friends are happy to stay at their home and have puppies but this was never an option for me and now sitting in my motorhome with Miffy's dust next to me I know that in her own way she is also experiencing this journey.

My only experience of seeing dust and the remains of a human body is linked to a person that came into my life a few years ago now. His name was Sidney Mount (Sid) was actually my step grandfather. He was known as Sid and was such a lovely guy, a real gentleman and he became part of my family when my mam remarried 16 years ago.

Sid used to live in Spain with his wife Pat and returned back to the UK due to ill health. After several tests he was diagnosed with prostate cancer and he battled this for many years, never complaining, defying science and managing to overcome countless episodes of radiotherapy treatments.

This treatment prolonged his life for many years after his initial diagnosis had only given him a few months to live.

Unfortunately his time came and he passed away aged 81 in a local hospice in Newcastle. His wish was for his body to be donated to science and this process began, as he was sent to the medical science department at Newcastle University.

Sid worked a policeman for many years in London and was as much of a character as the villains he used to enjoy telling us all about. He was quick witted and always had a joke or story to tell us about his life. Invariably some of the same tales were told time and time again but we always listened and showed interest even though we had heard them numerous times before.

The University carried out their research and then he was returned from the medical science department. Obviously in a different form as his body was cremated and his ashes returned to the family.

Around this time I visited my mams house with Ozzie and Roo and there he was, perched on the sideboard in what looked like a quality street jar the ones you get a Christmas, the tall ones with purple lids. It was a clear plastic jar so I could see the grey dust inside.

I picked the jar up to feel the weight of the ashes and to take a closer look. It felt heavy and I was surprised that there was so much ash in the jar. It just looked like the dust you see in the vacuum cleaner that collects in the cylinder as you hoover up. Regardless of who we are, what we do and what we look like, if we choose to be cremated this is how we all eventually end up.

Standing holding Sid's ashes I thought to myself, one day I will look like this too, just grey dust in a jar that then goes on to be placed somewhere in the house to collect even more dust. The dust in the jar has no personality, no witty comments like Sid used to provide, nothing at all, its just simply dust!

Without getting too morbid about this subject, I can now reflect on this and know this was a real trigger for me and turning point in my life. Maybe not a lightbulb moment but without doubt the cogs had slowly started to turn in my mind with me realising that I needed to start living my life doing what I wanted to do and not conforming to what others did or expected me to do.

My initial thoughts after putting Sid's ashes back on the sideboard were "what am I doing with my life?" Is my life colourful or am I grey and collecting dust, just like Sid's ashes.

I never thought of myself as the sort of person content to stay in a regular 9-5 job until I'm 65 years old working in order to get my pension by which time I may be in no fit state to enjoy this.

I knew I had to rebel against this dull beige life I had been existing in and start really living before I too become another statistic and turn to dust!

I myself, was very nearly dust only a few weeks prior to seeing Sid's ashes when Ozzie got me into a bit of a scrape. It was a usual occurrence that she stayed in the boot of the car whilst I drove and when I opened the boot she would sit and wait. On this occasion she didn't stop and wait and darted out of the boot and into the oncoming traffic in the road. Unfortunately as she darted out I grabbed her collar to try and stop her and in doing this she took me with her.

We were both in the middle of the road when a transit van sped past us so close in fact that I felt the tyres and warmth of the engine on my long hair. Still clutching Ozzie's collar I managed to roll back a few inches to get back onto the pavement. My friend Susie was with me at the time and was in shock, the colour drained from her face and she commented that she thought my time was up! My guardian angel must have been watching me that day and knew I had been lucky to have escaped my own death.

Following this I found myself repeatedly questioning and challenging myself on why I worked so hard, and what else was out there. Throughout my life I've always looked for contentment, striving to change things and make a better life for us all and my old life in the UK was just exhausting and to be honest it was hard work, so I knew that something had to change.

Paul and I had spent eighteen months travelling the world in 2002/3 and I thought the travel bug was out of my system. It clearly wasn't! I had always wanted to travel closer to home, and explore Europe but never really gave it too much thought as I was always so busy with my job that occupied all of my brain space. Seeing Sid's dull and grey ashes made something click in me that I had to do something different in my life and all I had to do was to convince Paul.

CHAPTER SIX

WHEELS IN MOTION

As expected Paul was reluctant to do the trip around Europe when I proposed it to him. He didn't want to go through the upheaval of packing up, selling the house, resigning from our jobs and eventually maybe having to return to Newcastle with no money, no home and start all over again. When I put down in words what I was asking him to do, I'm surprised that we actually made the decision to start the trip, especially when you add two energetic dogs into the equation.

This scenario had already played out when we returned from our eighteen month world trip in 2003. We arrived back in Newcastle penniless and then found that house prices had nearly trebled whilst we had been away. Back home with no money to speak of, we moved in for a few months with my dad and step mother. We found employment and worked as hard as we could to save money to help raise funds and then moved into a rented house not far from Newcastle City Centre. The hard work continued for another two years until we managed to save enough money for a deposit for our first home, and our dream home.

We were younger then, in our early 30's and accepted whatever situation we were faced with and just got on with it without a care in the world with no worries or stress. This time however, we were ten years older, knew the potential pitfalls and had to weigh these up against the positive benefits. I admit it felt scarier than last time, giving up steady jobs, great social lives, salaries, pensions and a very comfortable lifestyle in a beautiful home.

I needed to convince Paul and was persistent in my attempts. He would call this nagging! And at every opportunity I would nag! Sending him emails and texts with links to pictures of motorhomes or blogs of people who were living my dream and travelling Europe.

When out for drinks and meals I would look at the wine list and make comments that if we travelled we could go to the vineyard where the wine was produced which surely was better than drinking it in a bar. I would also act as though he had agreed and would talk about our future plans for a life on the road which included daily walks and runs in the sunshine! All of this fell on deaf ears but I didn't give up and kept making comments and nagging until he started coming around to the idea.

I'm guilty as charged and admit I did pester and bombard him with pleas to take the risk and go travelling. Paul does need to be pushed at times and he even admits this himself, so I knew I was doing the right thing at the right time as my gut instinct told me it was the right thing to do. Following my gut has always guided me in life and when making decisions if it feels right then I go with it. On the opposite end of the scale if it doesn't feel right then I don't do it.

In Newcastle we had a great life and were reasonably comfortable, earning good wages and had at least two or three holidays abroad every year. With a large group of friends at home who we had known for many years, leaving them and giving all of this up for a trip to Europe was at times a little overwhelming but just being short flight away gave me comfort and I hoped that friends could come and visit us which thankfully they have done.

Our wages were spent eating and drinking out on a weekly basis or buying the latest fashions and trends. Basically a disposable income that we easily managed to pour down the drain each month. We love to socialise and this at the time was our favourite past time. Every weekend was planned on where we would go out and party, either together or with a group of friends. Newcastle is known as the party capital of the UK with some amazing places to go to so this was hard to resist after a busy and at times stressful week at work. Come Friday, I couldn't wait to get out and let my hair down, dance on the tables, drink never ending glasses of red wine and release some of the pent up stress and energy I had collected during the seemingly endless meetings I had endured that week.

Whilst the thought of selling everything and packing up for a life on the road was completely new and out of the blue, we did have some limited experience of motorhoming. We had travelled through Australia and New Zealand in a campervan a few years ago and more recently had purchased our own VW campervan called Freda. We hadn't been seriously looking for a campervan although we were watching them on eBay to see what was available and how much they sold for. This changed when Paul came home after a Sunday afternoon in the pub to find out an item he was watching on the eBay auction was ending in an hour. After this there was only ever going to be one outcome.

We won the bid and drove to Kendal in the Lake District the following weekend to go and collect her. She was a 1986 T25 VW campervan and we immediately fell in love with her and Paul drove her home via the A69 with me, Ozzie and Roo following in our car closely behind. She seemed to be in decent condition for her age and we hoped she would only need a few tweaks here and there to get her in full working condition. Paul found the first job during the drive home when he realised the windscreen wipers didn't work which meant we had to keep stopping to wipe the rain away before continuing on. As you can imagine it took us quite a while to get home, though once there we were both rather pleased with ourselves when we replaced a fuse which made the wipers start working again. With little DIY or mechanical experience between us, we both soon managed to learn the basics and common ailments campervans have.

Our interest in campervans had been sparked by friends who had recently bought a VW campervan and told us of their weekends away and having Freda changed our weekends for the better. The days of finishing work and rushing to the pub or finishing work and putting the log burner on and relaxing for the evening were replaced with weekends spent in the lake district or exploring the coast of Northumberland. Even when we didn't go away for the weekend we would head out on Sunday mornings to the coast at Druridge bay to meet Dean, Dawn and their daughter Charlotte for breakfast in their campervan which was a top of the range Brazilian imported VW named Douglas. This was a campervan with all the bells and whistles on and included a Union Jack roof which made poor old Freda look like a clapped out antique parked next to him.

A brisk walk on the beach always ended with breakfast back at Freda with usually bacon, egg and sausage in soft white bread buns. Regardless of the weather, breakfast at the beach was always a joy and warmed us on the inside even if it was sometimes blowing a gale and freezing outside.

Freda was old and rusty in places but all things considered she was in pretty good shape for a thirty year old and after owning her for four months we decided to take her on her first road trip to a place Paul and I had always wanted to visit. Some years earlier we had read an article about the Isle of Skye and vowed that one day we would go. That time was now and during Easter 2014 we packed her up, made the dogs comfortable in the back, closed and locked all doors and cupboards and set off on the 360 mile journey to Skye.

If you're expecting a horror story here about breaking down, being stranded or hating life in Freda you'll be disappointed as she was fantastic and didn't let us down at all. The fuel consumption left a lot to be desired but apart from that she was faultless.

With wild camping permitted in Scotland we loved the freedom of driving each day and parking up somewhere new and free each evening. As this was a holiday and as Freda still needed work to get the fridge and water operational we ate out each evening and spent our nights talking to locals in pubs and restaurants, receiving recommendations on where to go to the following day. This recommendation method and not planning worked a treat and everywhere we visited was solely based on where we were recommended to go the previous evening which worked out perfectly.

Mother nature also played her part as each day was warm with clear blue skies and thankfully no rain. Having ten days in Scotland with no rain is considered something of a miracle.

Highlights of the trip included Dunvegan's coral beach on Skye which ranks as one of the most beautiful we have ever visited. It was April and deserted which only added to the appeal. I can imagine however that it doesn't look as beautiful in the middle of August when no doubt it is over run with tourists.

Our route back to Newcastle took us to The Claighaig Inn at Glencoe. Here we spent two days walking the mountains during the day and talking to the locals by the fire in the pub each night and we listened to the traditional tunes from the local folk band that frequented both evenings. We both loved this lifestyle and having the freedom to do anything we wanted made us feel alive and excited to explore more.

For a split second I did entertain the idea of using Freda for our planned trip to Europe but deep down I knew she wasn't reliable enough for the distances we intended. She didn't have enough space for all four of us nor any showering facilities. Plus the amount of petrol she guzzled would have bankrupted us and would have us back in the UK within weeks.

The wheels really started moving with an impromptu meeting with my cousin who I hadn't seen in over twenty years. Paul and I joined John and his partner Kate for drinks in a wine bar in the centre of Newcastle and we celebrated this reunion with copious amounts of alcohol. When Paul and I went out in town we would drop Ozzie and Roo off to stay with our friends Amy and Kevin who lived in the centre of Newcastle. Both dogs loved staying there and looked forward to their walks in the Newcastle Bigg Market eating scraps of kebab meat and pizza left over from the revellers the night before.

Back in the wine bar with my long lost cousin and after the initial catch up with one another talking about what we had all been up to over the years we started to talk about the future and the plans and ideas I had in mind. During the conversation Paul started to make comments that sounded like he was actually thinking about going travelling. I had drank plenty of wine so wasn't 100% sure what I was hearing but it certainly sounded like he was starting to come round to all of the nagging and earache I had been giving him about wanting to travel Europe.

The seed was planted and sprouting! Hooray... and more wine was drunk...!

The following day Paul started researching the many facets needed to make this trip a possibility and began to make enquiries into buying a motorhome and also made comments to his friends and family about travelling and places in Europe. Over the coming weeks we thought about the logistics of making a trip of this magnitude and the procedures for getting pet passports for the dogs and travel insurance for us which really excited me knowing that this was now going to be a definite trip. I needed to keep the momentum going and booked an appointment at the vets for the following day where in under twenty minutes we left with two pet passports and full health checks.

This is probably a good time to mention that our house had been up for sale for ten months. Initially we simply wanted somewhere slightly larger. A house in the same area with a bigger kitchen and garden for the dogs. We had a young couple who wanted to buy our house, however we couldn't find anywhere that met our criteria. Some people would see this as an issue, whereas I saw it as an omen. With Paul now agreeing to the idea of travelling abroad, a buyer for our house was the final piece of the jigsaw.

We used to be a fairly organised couple but on this occasion everything seemed to engulf us. We had both been busy with tying up loose ends at work and on top of that we had to fit in selling a house, packing up all of our belongings, selling our car, and buying a larger more suitable motorhome for our trip.

With a week to go before the contracts were due to be exchanged all of the above were still on our to-do list. Moving house is difficult enough without having to factor in finding storage for all of our possessions. Despite several viewings on eBay and at local garages we were unable to find a motorhome that was suitable for us and within our budget.

If you discount the North Shields to Amsterdam ferry then Newcastle is a long way from most of the UK ferry ports leading into Europe. It's possibly for this reason that motorhomes and motorhome dealers are in short supply in the North East of England. Paul and I scoured the internet desperately looking for a motorhome that would meet all of our requirements. As we only had a few days now to go until we were going to be homeless, we had to do something.

We saw a private sale in Wallsend and as this was only five miles from our home we arranged a viewing for Thursday 3rd July 2014. It was a 2005 Fiat Ducato Ci Carioca and looked to be in good condition. The owners had bought it two years previously and had planned to use it for trips around the UK but family reasons had prevented them using it at all. Whilst it was in great condition there was a problem in that we didn't like the layout. It had an overhead sleeping cab, which was fine, it was the seating area(s) that was the problem. Behind the driver seat was a table which was surrounded by seats. Behind this towards the rear was a toilet area and another table surrounded by more seating. I haven't worked out why there was a need to have two tables and two separate seating areas.

The condition and age ticked our boxes, as did the price, but the layout was causing us to query whether this was the motorhome for us. We decided to sleep on it, thanked the owners for their time and marked it down as a possible.

The following day, and four days before we were due to hand over our keys to the new owners of 11 Park View, Paul and his friends headed off to Reeth for the Tour de France. Talk about timing! He took Freda and also left me to do the majority of the packing of all our possessions. This consisted of throwing out a load of clutter I had consumed over the years from the countless car boot sales and markets I liked to go to. It felt great getting rid of all of this clutter I had been storing, it really was rubbish and as I cleared I left various items outside in the front garden with a note saying 'free to good home'. This worked well and within minutes all soon disappeared, going to neighbours close by, for them to clutter their homes with.

I had managed to pack a good few boxes when Paul returned from Reeth on the Sunday afternoon and within a few minutes of getting home he went into meltdown mode. The realisation of what we were doing, and how much we still had to do hit home and he panicked. We had two days to pack up the remainder of our stuff and find homes for it all, plus we still needed to buy a motorhome that would take us around Europe.

We woke on Monday morning and knew that the Fiat Ducato was our only option. In twenty four hours we would be homeless and we accepted that travelling Europe in a motorhome would be impossible if we didn't have a motorhome to do it in. Thankfully the Fiat hadn't been snapped up over the weekend and we agreed to pay £13,000 and pick it up later that day.

Looking back we made every mistake you could think of. Lack of research, insufficient knowledge, running out of time and leaving ourselves with no plan B. The only thing we got right was the price. Buying off an auction site, from people who originally had similar intentions to us before other factors got in the way for them, meant we had negotiated a good deal.

When we collected the motorhome we started the engine and drove it away and found it very different to driving Freda (which was still up for sale in our driveway). At seven metres it felt huge and had no back window which made it really challenging to manoeuvre. We drove it home to fill it with all of our belongings and friends neighbours all came out to see it. The dogs jumped in and gave it a good inspection and sniffed every inch of it then settled in the front seats where they could look out.

My mam named our new motorhome Teddy due to it having a large quiff at the front. This quiff is the bedroom part over on the cabin and reminded her of a 1960's Teddy boy's hairstyle, slicked back with tons of brylcream, nowadays this quiff is slicked back with copious amounts of pollyfilla due to the bumps, scrapes and cracks it has encountered on its journey.

With the motorhome purchased it was now all hands to the deck with family and friends all helping with the last push to empty the house and without their help we would have been in trouble.

With our bedroom furniture dismantled and sent off to storage we threw some cushions onto the bedroom floor and spent our last night in an empty house wondering what the future would hold. Monday had been a productive day and our to-do list was getting shorter by the minute and all of the major tasks had been achieved with one notable exception. We hadn't managed to sell Freda. A couple of last minute offers came in for her but they were so ridiculously low that they hadn't warranted a discussion.

With time running out we made the decision to keep Freda and put her into storage and we spent the Tuesday morning filling her with the last items from the house and drove her to the storage yard tucking her in amongst all the other homeless campervans. Saying our farewells was emotional, silly I know as she is just a campervan but we had grown attached to her. So now she sits in the yard awaiting our return.

The new house owners arrived just as we were moving some essentials into our new motorhome (Teddy). We handed the keys to them and said goodbye to our lovely home for the last time. We had moved there in 2005 on our wedding anniversary and spent nine happy years in Wideopen but we both knew we were ready to embark on the next chapter of our lives.

After a tearful goodbye to our home we made our way to our refuge for our final night in Newcastle. This was six doors along from our old house, the one we had just vacated. Our neighbours and friends Derek and Dorothy provided us with a bed for the night and treated us to 5 star accommodation, welcoming us with a home cooked breakfast/brunch which is one of Dorothy's specialties. Derek made us a gorgeous meal in the evening and Paul and I were exhausted and went to bed shortly afterwards, both of us looking forward to the following day and the excitement of the unknown territory that we now faced.

I sensed for a while that something was happening as furniture was being taken out of the house and we all spent the night at number 5 Park View, Derek and Dorothy's house.

For years we have had the same daily routine. First Emma would wake up and then she would open the bedroom door to let Roo and I in where we jumped up onto the bed snuck under the quilt and had a cuddle.

I loved this part of the day as I was always excited to see Paul and Emma after being asleep for so long. I used to wake through the night and go and check to see if they were awake but they never were. Yet at the same time each day, when the room filled with light, I knew it was nearly time to get in with them.

After cuddles Roo and I would be taken out for a long walk before Paul and Emma had to go to work. Emma to a place two miles down the road, Paul upstairs into his office. Morning walks were my favourite as it meant I could go and release the energy I had built up all night.

The mornings were always cooler too and especially in the spring time I loved to run through the long wet grass feeling the coolness on my stomach. We would then go home, eat our breakfast and then sleep until lunchtime where we had another, shorter, walk. We were familiar with this routine, liked it and had done it for years.

It was the same routine when Miffy was alive. Sometimes humans and other dog friends would call around to see us but apart from that Roo and I knew exactly what was coming and at what time and when. All of our walks and meals were structured which made us happy and content.

I'm not really sure what work is as I've never had to do any, but work was a word Emma used when she left us in the mornings. This work word was our trigger for us to get back into our beds and sleep. Emma would shout "I'm going to work" and within seconds Roo and I were curled up in our beds and preparing for another few hours' snooze.

Roo and I enjoyed this peace, quiet and relaxation time, though we also loved it when Emma arrived home. Call it sixth sense but we would know when she was getting closer. We would run upstairs, into the front room, climb on top of the storage chest and look out of the window straining our necks to be the first to see the car pull up and then Emma climbing out. This first glimpse of her sent us into a state of excitement as her arrival would mean lots of cuddles and treats. She always makes a fuss of us and there was always lots of toys to play with and treat after treat just kept coming out of our favourite cupboard.

So back to being in the wrong house and I was still wondering why we were sleeping at Derek and Dorothy's and why we weren't going back to our home? I looked at Roo, she looked at me and I felt anxious and more than a little confused.

The next morning I was exhausted as I had been worrying all night and had little sleep. Roo had been flat out and she woke just as Paul and Emma stirred. After our walk I straining on my lead to go to our familiar home but we went back to number five for breakfast and then were taken into the larger vehicle that we had sniffed out yesterday which I now know to be called a motorhome, basically a house on wheels.

The motorhome was like a smaller version of our house and a larger version of Freda. It had our cushions, curtains and blankets in it from our home. It felt like our house but I knew it couldn't be as it moved. I had a good sniff around and jumped into the passenger seat to get a better view of everything around us and from there I could see all the people outside looking at us and waving us goodbye.

Paul put the key in the ignition and started the engine which was very loud and made me jump. He closed the doors and then we started to move exactly like the car does though this was very noisy. Roo and I sat on the seats behind Paul and Emma and we got bumped from one side to the next crashing into each other as it moved. Things kept making noises above us and then objects would fall out of cupboards and land on our heads. Teething problems were the words coming from the front seats.

This initial journey didn't last too long and when we stopped I was thankful for the chance to get out. It felt strange and made me feel sick and Roo and I were fed up with being a target for things dropping on us from above.

Being an observant Beagle I am always very aware of my surroundings and knew most of my local area so I was surprised to see that I hadn't been to this place before. There were plenty of other oversized cars and a few tents pegged to the ground. I guessed it was a campsite and we'd stayed at these before in Freda. As soon as the doors opened Roo and I raced off like we usually do and darted through fields, streams and over hedges. Although we had only been in the motorhome for an hour Roo and I were relieved to be out and happy to be free as we ran wild through the fields close by.

I could smell rabbits, foxes and deer and it was great. My legs were stretched out with my hind legs kicking back and the wind blowing through my ears as I raced as fast as I could. Roo was close behind me and struggled to keep up. She is much faster over short distances but doesn't have my stamina and sometimes lags behind on longer sprints. I should wait for her, but never do, I was off and into the hills now and sniffing out the scent of rabbits that had been there. Mmmm delicious, there was rabbit poo and I grabbed mouthfuls of this as I ran by. This was doggy caviar at its best.

When I eventually returned to the motorhome after eating poo to bursting point I was feeling good in myself and energized and had forgotten all about the awful journey we had getting here. As the night unfolded and darkness arrived I sensed that perhaps we were actually going away and travelling in this thing that I now know as Teddy. Bed time came and I couldn't believe it when Paul and Emma got a ladder out and climbed upstairs to their bed. Roo and I didn't know where to settle, where we were supposed to lie and

I mentally prepared myself for another sleepless night. I wanted to go home, back to Park View, wrapped in a blanket on a nice warm cosy sofa in front of the fire that I could still imagine, with cinders glowing and heating the room but I knew I had to be brave at this point.

Instead I'm in a motorhome and trying to work out where was going to be the most comfortable place to sleep. I decided to try the front seat and managed to settle there for a while. Listening to Roo snoozing peacefully beside me I sat awake for several hours and watched the sky turn from night to day and tried to work out what on earth was happening.

The next day arrived and my deep thoughts through the night made me understand that this was my new life. My days used to have structure, and a comfortable bed but now I'm balanced on a small seat that is hard, lumpy and smells different. I gave myself a shake and told myself to be brave as I knew things could be worse. I could be dust just as Miffy is now, at least I still have my life, my freedom and my favourite people around me.

I reflected on the previous days and although I wasn't sure exactly what was ahead of me I knew life had changed, possibly forever and hopefully for the better. I looked at Roo who had encountered no difficulty in getting her recommended eight hours sleep. She looked happy and content as she always does and part of me wishes I was as laid back as her.

I heard a sound above me, then movement and I then saw some familiar legs just dangle in front of my face, as Paul made his way down the ladder. He hugged me and gave me a kiss which cheered me up and was a nice little touch to start my day. He sat down and I moved to sit with him as it was warmer where he was and as I sat with my head on his lap I could sense that he was happy. I rested my paw on his arm while he gave me more cuddles. This was affection Ozzie style and was my only method of communication that he understands.

I looked around trying to figure out our next move and I could see some of the other motorhomes moving off. I heard Emma's voice high above me and I strained my neck to catch a glimpse of her but couldn't see her. Within minutes she climbed down the ladder and then hugged and kissed us all. Roo always gets extra excited when she sees Emma and always gets the first and longest cuddle. The same is true of me and Paul. I look beyond Emma to see where she has been sleeping and realise that the days of grabbing five minutes in their bed are over. There is no way that we, or any other dog, could manage to climb, up there, no matter how much we stretch up and stand on our tippy claws.

Moving out of our house was as stressful as it is for most people but thankfully it was over fairly quickly. Our motorhome is now our new home, and our transport and our first night was spent staying on a small site near Richmond in Yorkshire. Packing up and leaving Newcastle all in under seventy two hours was intense as we adapted to our new life in Teddy with a somewhat limited floor space.

Not getting in each other's way and finding a home for everything took some time and some getting used to. Our bed is in the roof on top of the drivers' cabin and it is very snug to say the least. Our first night consisted of us banging our heads, knees and elbows and found out that thankfully we do not suffer from claustrophobia. The roof is low and we are used to it now but it is extremely cramped up there with barely any room to turn. The dogs haven't got a clue what is going on and they are dying to have a look at our sleeping area. Roo spent some of this morning standing with her head raised high and nose in the air sniffing to try and find us. Both dogs are used to the finer things in life and as much as we enjoy a morning snuggle with them I don't think all four of us could fit in the bed now. It's a tight squeeze as it is.

Ozzie has found her comfortable place in the passenger seat and seems to be adapting quite well. It's called a captain's chair and swivels allowing her to face us when we are sitting in the rear lounge. A constant worry when deciding to make this trip was how the dogs would find it, and how they would adapt. Would they enjoy it or get too stressed and hate travelling in a motorhome? This is especially true of Ozzie who as you know, thinks travelling should be done using only her four little legs.

Our first night accomplished, we packed up the motorhome, though as we hadn't reached the site until late there wasn't much to put away. Just before leaving I noticed the rear tyre was low on air, very low on air. Despite my lack of mechanic training I identified this as a possible puncture. Limping out of the campsite we drove for 10-15 minutes before finding a garage. It would have been quicker if we had thought about bringing with us a sat nav or map but leaving Newcastle in a hurry and being completely disorganised was already coming back to bite us.

Thankfully we found a garage who had good news, bad news and bad, bad news. Yes, we had a puncture, yes they could repair it, and unfortunately we required four new tyres. They estimated that the motorhome had been standing for some time without use and the tyres had started to crack, causing a weakness common in motorhomes and caravans.

This was true and backed up the story from the previous owners about its lack of use. The two mechanics said we may get away with this if we were embarking on a short trip. How long were we away for? The answer, forever, was memorable in two ways. Firstly the look of disbelief on their faces and secondly the realisation of what we were actually embarking on.

It also meant that our travelling fund was about to be depleted before we had exited the North, never mind the UK. The bad, bad news was that they would have to order in the new tyres and they wouldn't be available until that afternoon. Quickly weighing up the safety implications we ordered four new tyres and wandered around Richmond for what was a very pleasant afternoon. We returned around 4pm, new tyres had arrived, quickly fitted and off we went, promising the two very pleasant tyre fitters a mention in our book, should we ever write it and get it published. There you go guys.

Our next planned stop was Cambridge. We had passed through this area a few years earlier on day 1 of a skiing trip around Europe and as it was on our route towards Dover it made sense to head there. The lack of a sat nav and getting Teddy stuck in the university car park put paid to that idea and we pulled up at the nearest campsite that was on the outskirts of the city. On route we stopped off at a shop for some supplies of food and drinks and on returning to Teddy noticed a rather large dint in his side panel and part of the bumper on the ground. Whilst shopping someone had very kindly bumped their car into us and drove off without letting us know. Picking the bumper up and taping the remainder of the panel with some gaffa tape, we continued on. This dint and lack of bumper ended up seeing us through most of our trip and on a positive note at least we had our tyres now! We were making progress, but I had to admit it was slow and sporadic progress.

We had friends in Hornchurch who invited us to stay on our way south. The offer was kind, it was on our way down to Dover and would allow us a night or two out of the motorhome and check what we have and what we needed. Maybe that should read what we haven't and we need everything.

Another factor to consider here was that they live above a pub on the high street in Hornchurch. I was thinking that the chances of getting Paul, Teddy and the dogs to Dover were decreasing by the minute.

However, a couple of nights out of the motorhome and a chance to see friends proved too much and we spent a very enjoyable two nights with them. We visited Hornchurch both evenings and we found a huge disused airfield within walking distance to exercise the dogs that was frequented by foxes. It was interesting to see the relationship between them and the dogs. The dogs being terrified of them and running in the opposite direction away from them but at the same time showing curiosity between each other.

Whilst there Paul bought a sat nav which he said would save years of our time and also many arguments which he was right about and we also invested in a much needed European map. Again these are things many consider essentials and we really should have bought these before leaving Newcastle.

From Hornchurch we headed towards Kent and visited Broadstairs which is where we found a problem with our water heating system. Sometimes it worked, sometimes it didn't. As we were staying on a campsite, we asked around for help and advice as we believed we must be doing something wrong. A couple of friendly neighbours came and looked at our heating system and after much pulling, prodding and reading manuals they confirmed that we were doing everything correctly. Nice to hear we were not completely hopeless, although the water still only heated up when it wanted to. This was yet another problem we had that we were fearful would eat into our budget and we hadn't even crossed the channel yet!

CHAPTER SEVEN

AND WE'RE OFF

It took us one week from moving out of our home in Newcastle to get to the docks at Dover ferry terminal. Once arrived, we checked in and sat waiting in a queue of other motorhomes waiting for our ferry crossing to Calais. It was 1.30 in the afternoon and we watched as all the other people waited in their cars around us wondering what their stories were and where they were going.

Whilst waiting I made us some sandwiches for the trip whilst being closely observed by Roo who watched my every move desperately hoping for a small crumb to fall. This, we have found, is one of the bonuses of having a motorhome where we can eat on the go and save time stopping off to eat. Nowadays I often make lunch whilst Paul is driving and it makes us laugh as I try to balance myself getting the food from the fridge and onto the table, then the task of making a half decent edible sandwich whilst we manoeuvred around corners and bumps, the roundabouts being the most trickiest of feats. This usually results with the ham, cheese and tomatoes flying into the air which sends Roo launching at them so you can imagine it can be a little chaotic. My skills however have improved and I have even mastered the skill of going to the loo whilst in transit again and all to save time when on a long journey.

Back to the docks in Dover where Paul and I sat in the queue of traffic and this gave us time to reflect on the past week and what has brought us to being there. Selling our home of nine years, packing up our belongings, relying on friends, family and neighbours to look after us and store our belongings. Picking up a motorhome that we knew nothing about, saying our goodbyes and now wondering what was lying ahead of us and what our next chapter in life would involve, became quite overwhelming for us both. The gates opened and we were ushered through and onto the ferry, no turning back now and a smooth 90 minute crossing took us to France.

Our first few nights spent in the motorhome meant we were still finding things in Teddy that we didn't know existed. Such as a control panel on the wall that tells us if batteries are charged and water is full. Although we had read the manual to try and understand this, it was so complicated we just found it easier to ignore any flashing lights or symbols that appeared. We thought we would be familiar with all of the contraptions in the motorhome after having Freda but we were wrong and after crossing through France and into Belgium we noticed that there was a really awful smell in Teddy and we couldn't work out what it was or where it was coming from.

The smell got worse when we were in transit and I would ask Paul to pull over and stop and sniff around to try and find where it was coming from. This awful stench went on for days and days and was getting worse. At each stop we inspected Teddy and I bought detergent to clean the floors walls and ceilings but still the smell was there. It reminded me of a mixture of damp dirty dish cloths and rotten eggs mixed with boiled vegetables, it really was a gut retching odour.

We couldn't stand the smell any longer and pulled into a site in Bruges for the night. It was a hot humid evening and yes the smell was still with us. Once we got parked up I had a shower in the 1ft by 1ft shower cubicle in the motorhome, a tight squeeze for anyone. I could hear Paul outside having a very loud conversation/argument with an Italian gentleman that had parked next to us. He sounded annoyed and the translation of Italian I could make out was that we had water leaking from somewhere. Hearing this conversation was getting heated I hurried to get dry and put some clothes on to get out to help defuse the situation. Once outside my hair still dripping wet the Italian man was pointing to the back of our motorhome and underneath it explaining that there is a tank that collects all of the waste water which needs to be emptied. It was then that it clicked that this must have been where all of our waste water had been collecting! We had never given it any thought as to where this was going and in approaching two weeks it had never been emptied, as we didn't know it was there.

The tank was obviously, by this time, full to bursting point and therefore had started to leak and was incredibly smelly. Unfortunately we weren't the most popular people on site that night. The smell was awful and very embarrassing. Where did we think all of the water from the sink and shower was going? Evaporating? As Teddy was parked up for the night and the excess water had drained away with no more leaks, we did the sensible thing, got ready and went to the pub! Not for the beer of course, though Belgium beers are high on the list of our favourites, just so we could discuss how on earth you empty the tank.

The following morning and another review of the manual we found the section about the catch that opens the tank to dispose of what is known as grey water. After observing the other motorhomers there was a drain close by that you lifted and then you manoeuvre your motorhome over it to empty. You can imagine the stench and the wide berth we received as we released the catch to rid two weeks' worth of water. Thankfully, the grey water situation had been explained to us and the toilet cassette had received a regular empty and clean too. Before we left I said farewell to our Italian neighbours and a bottle of wine and two kisses on each cheek left us on a good note but deep down we knew he was pleased to see the back of us.

Our sat nav programmed for our next stop sent us off in completely the wrong direction. The coordinates programmed in were supposed to be taking us to another camping spot in Belgium but instead took us to a military practice firing range. Connie the sat nav as we now called her had taken us off piste, along baron tracks through barriers and into unauthorised territory. We questioned the possibility that it may have been the wrong way but kept our trust and faith with Connie who on this occasion let us down badly. Being spotted by senior guards who were alerted that there was a British motorhome looking very lost on site raised alarm bells and we were soon shown the exit and escorted off their land.

We drove around and around for hours and I knew we were lost as every time I looked out of the window it was familiar and we passed the same places time and time again. Thankfully a man appeared and we were shown how to get out and then we were back on the main road.

We arrived at our spot for the night and as it was late we all went straight to bed and slept soundly until the wind started to howl outside which then started to rock us and this is one of the many things I detest. Yes my anxiety started to appear again and this grew stronger and worries me more and more as the winds outsides picked up and howled around us.

It was blowing a gale outside and the trees above us showered their branches on us making an almighty racket. Thankfully the winds woke Paul and Emma and we had to drive off to a sheltered area only a few yards up the road which in itself was a challenge. Some of the trees around us had fallen and Teddy had to do his best to manoeuvre around these. Once settled in our new and less exposed spot for the night although still troubled by the wind but not as much we all rested and slept until early morning. Where we woke to the sound of busy activity around us. It was market day in this part of Belgium and all of the traders had started to set up their stalls around us. Unbeknown to us we had parked obstructing the pedestrian access for the market. I have never see Emma move as fast she jumped from the cabin above and still in her pyjamas started up Teddy and we drove off.

Our final night in Belgium resulted in us being engulfed in one of the windiest storms we've ever experienced and we decided to move at 4am, as the trees around us were falling and we didn't want one to topple on us. Due to being disorientated at this hour and unfamiliar with the area we didn't realise that we had actually parked right in the middle of the market square. By 7am the storm had eased somewhat and the chaos of market day surrounded us. Literally hundreds of people around us were busy setting up for the day and we were clearly in their way. Obviously we had to move fast which we did. Again this is a lesson we've learnt when wild camping to make sure it is in a safe area away from trees and not blocking any access. So onwards we drove, well this time I was driving, still in my pyjamas and in no time we arrived in another new country, Holland.

CHAPTER EIGHT

BRATWURSTS AND BICYCLES

After once again finding ourselves lost, we managed to find a motorhome stop in Holland where we based ourselves for a few nights. We may have had Connie with us but using her is another matter. Our previous experience of minutes and seconds were through watches.

It was a nice clean site and the owners were friendly and showed us local maps of walks and the popular places to visit in the area. When touring in a motorhome we never really know where we are going to end up as so many things can get in the way and you have probably gathered that we don't really do planning. It really has just been through google searches and a bit of luck that we've found places to stop or campsites to stay on for the night. We have however found that these vary in quality, facilities and price. It wasn't until we reached Holland that we met a fellow motorhomer who told us of an app you can get called camper contact that shows all the campsites across Europe and this is what we use now and has been a godsend to us. Although we had never planned our route around Europe we just sort of expected to take on board other people's recommendations and advice of where to visit and where to go next. From now, most evenings would be spent looking at our map and then cross referencing this with advice we had sought from others or google searches.

Holland was a pleasant stop for a few days, a pretty country where everyone gets from one place to the next by bike. Thousands of bikes in fact and they are everywhere which is great for the environment and personal fitness but one that also presents a hazard for dogs and walkers alike. Caution is needed especially when visiting cities such as Amsterdam which has around 800,000 bikes.

Wherever we went sounds of bells and horns echoed the air as countless and endless cyclists swerved and dodged past us. As it's very flat in Holland it is considered ideal for cycling but bikes and I don't get on and despite having brought our bikes with us, mine remained gathering rust and tied to the back of Teddy. Oddly enough, I can run for miles and miles but find it incredibly difficult and exhausting to cycle. I once spent three days cycling the C2C route in England from Workington to Tynemouth and this put me off for life.

One thing I did notice was that all ages were cycling past us at an impressive speed including the older generations. On closer inspection I noticed that an increasing number of these bikes are now battery operated making it easier to ride as I was puzzled as to how unbelievably fast some of the more elderly riders raced past us! This kind of cycling appeals to me though the price tag attached to these bikes take them out of our budget at this time.

This was getting really annoying now all I wanted to do was walk but these ridiculous bicycles were getting in my way. My back leg was caught by one of the tyres that ran into me and there were just hundreds of these heading for me in all directions. I heard the bells that warned us but they go so fast that I didn't get a moment to get out of the way. I was constantly on guard, whipped up into a frenzy and moving from side to side. The sharp sound of the screeching brakes was a familiar noise and this generally made me freeze which usually resulted in me getting hit or shouted at. Having had enough of this madness and inability to enjoy a walk without the interference of bicycles I was pleased to hear that Holland was especially popular with bicycles and this wouldn't be a problem once we moved into other countries so I was keen to get on the move again.

We were itching to keep on going with our travels and with no firm plans of a route in place we took the next logical route to Germany which we were really looking forward to. Paul being a big fan of Auf Wiedersehen Pet, we wanted to see if there was anything there that reminded him of the show. This is Pauls' favourite programme of all time, so much so, that he knows every word of every single episode in every series and obviously has a connection to this with Oz, Dennis and Neville characters of the show being from Newcastle. I brought a little bit of Auf Wiedersehen Pet to Teddy and have named all of the cupboards after the different characters from the show. This makes it easier to find things which is a regular activity as living in a motorhome you are constantly looking for things! I've lost count of the times we say to each other "where is this" and "where is that". There are so many cupboards in Teddy so when Paul asks where a certain thing is now I can say they are in Barry or Wayne as opposed to third one along and second on the right. The wine glasses are kept in Oz and the pots and pans are kept in Dennis. The more boring items are kept in Neville.

We soon found out how accessible Europe was and within only a couple of hours of leaving Amsterdam we had crossed the border and arrived in Germany, stopping at a lovely small town called Bad Bentheim. Our first impressions of Germany were very impressive with clean, motorhome stops that were well sign-posted. Designated and spacious parking places and water filling, all in pristine condition. The sites in Germany were very well looked after and catered for the needs of motorhomers which makes it an enjoyable place to stay.

We found that there was an air of sophistication in Germany with lots of traditional and stylish cafes and restaurants that were all dog friendly, something we had heard about years ago and in some parts they even allow dogs in supermarkets. One downfall that we found is that most establishments hadn't yet discovered Wi-Fi but as its only 2015 they have plenty of time to catch up. The locals were friendly too and everyone we met made us feel very welcome. The whole place was just immaculate, their pride in cleanliness really shone through.

Arriving at Bad Bentheim on our fourteenth Wedding anniversary, we wanted to find a place where we could celebrate. We pulled into the local stellplatz. As mentioned above this is a place where motorhomes are allowed to stay for the night. There was an electric hook up which we plugged in and turned our fridge on to keep our champagne chilled for later that evening.

There was just us and two other motorhomes parked up, a German motorhome and one from the Netherlands so we felt safe to leave Teddy and explore the place. We headed towards the town and literally forty yards from where we parked we stumbled across a small restaurant that looked inviting. It was around 5pm and still hot in the sun, though turning cold in the shade we wanted to get warm somewhere. We wandered in and the place was totally empty, not a soul there apart from a young guy stood behind the bar. This being our first visit to a German bar with dogs in tow we asked if they were allowed. Absolutely, or the German equivalent, was the reply.

We requested two cold beers which he served us, though we did notice that he half-filled over ten pint glasses just to get our two pints. The beer from the pumps was so frothy and milky that to get the beer he had to try this on numerous attempts! From removing the froth from one, to adding some more beer into another, then repeated, though this time removing froth from a different glass and refilling another. I initially thought that incompetence had played a part yet I have seen this repeated many times within German bars. Why? I haven't had the heart, or courage to ask. Beers in hand we felt content with the coolness of the lager and the warmth of the surroundings we were in.

The silence of the bar was soon broken when a man walked in and this took the number of patrons to three but his presence and personality was a welcome addition to the bar and it felt as though he alone had filled the whole room. Anst was his name and we got chatting to him about the food menu which had a variety of dishes containing words that we simply couldn't make out. His English was excellent and helped us with this. He had lived in the area all his life and used to be a teacher at the local school. He told us about the history of the small town, where to go, what to see and the best dog walking routes. He was a real lively character and had a warm friendly face that I instantly liked.

He recommended we try some food from the menu which he translated for us. In summary all dishes contained an eclectic mix of sausages in various forms and sauces. We wanted to try traditional dishes in every country and we associate the Bratwurst sausage to Germany so we booked a table for later that evening. We then proceeded to the next bar which then led us to the next and the next. All as friendly and welcoming as the first and all with the ritual of requiring at least ten glasses to pour two beers.

Each bar we visited had sausages on offer with different sauces and by this time our bellies were full to bursting of beer and bratwursts and our champagne was still waiting for us being by this time very chilled. As we had already overdosed on sausage we amended our reservation at the restaurant for the following evening, headed back to Teddy and enjoyed our champagne clinking our glasses to celebrate fourteen years of marriage.

Anst told us of a nice walk which we did the following day and it took us through some wooded areas to the next town, and back again. About six miles in total, this was our first decent walk in Germany and led us past what looked like a spa/hotel with lots, and lots of elderly people enjoying the pool and surrounding area. An encounter with Anst later that day told us that this was a place that specialised in treating those with the psoriasis skin condition as the waters had special healing powers. There were so many elderly people there all bathing in the healing waters, the movie Cocoon immediately sprang to mind! My next thought was to wonder who had the unfortunate job of cleaning the water filters of the pool!

After a few days in Bad Bentheim we continued onto our next destination and packed Teddy up and off we went, heading north was our only plan. Not knowing what road to take or where to go next really is all part of the adventure.

We came across a beautiful harbour town called Emden where by chance there was a traditional dragon boat racing event happening, right next to where the motorhomes parked up. The familiar smell of barbequed bratwurst filled the air and this led us to a perfect spot right at the front of the harbour so we had the best seats in the house to watch the weekend long event. It was a nice small friendly town and whilst there we managed to stock up on some supplies including the traditional bratwurst, because since being here we had developed a liking for these. Just as well really as we found there was limited choice of foods in Germany. We did eat lots of these in Germany as we found them to be very adaptable sausages, ideal to be enjoyed for breakfast, lunch and dinner. Variations of bratwurst sandwiches, bratwurst and rice, bratwurst soup and pasta and our firm favourite the curried bratwurst. The dogs too became accustomed to our food choice and goodness knows how many we chomped our way through whilst there.

"Give me the sausage" I pleaded, putting my really cute face on as I begged for more Bratwurst and then a small morsel of sausage fell to the ground that I could eat. These sausages are so good, might I say even better than my all-time favourite, tuna fish. Roo and I were given large portions of these sausages which we adored as Emma likes us to try the different foods from the places we visit. We had snails in France, Bitterballen in Holland, various tapas in Spain but this sausage beats them all.

From Emden we drove to Hamburg and the motorhome stop there was very basic, in an industrial area on the outskirts of the city but it served its purpose for a stay there to explore. Being in a city with a motorhome and two dogs presents different challenges and the dogs aren't used to getting on and off trains and buses but this was our only method of transport to explore this vast area.

This was also Roo's first encounter with an escalator which completely freaked her out. As we approached it I felt the lead tighten and she pulled back resisting and wouldn't move. By this time Paul and Ozzie had carried on onto the escalator and were nearing the top but I couldn't budge Roo. After several attempts to get her to step on to it she grew impatient and promptly made a run for it taking me with her at a ground breaking speed literally reaching the top and being reunited with Paul and Ozzie within seconds.

Paul and I kept thinking to ourselves what must be going through the mind of Ozzie and Roo during these first weeks of our trip as we are constantly on the move, in such a confined space, whereas at home they were settled and in a routine, always knowing what was coming next. In Newcastle their days were mapped out so they knew when walks were going to happen and when I would be due home from work and most importantly when mealtimes were.

Realising they were so out of their routine we were so proud of them for adapting to this new way of life. There was no plan B, so if they had not been so adaptable and accommodating who knows what would have happened if they had turned their noses up at a life on the road. Of the two, I would say Roo is enjoying herself the most, she wags her tail constantly and has so much energy, she is so alive and is always full of high spirits. Ozzie on the other hand still has some work to do to relax into it. She is confused, her facial expressions remain a mix of fear and dread, constantly on alert or worrying about the wind outside or any other strange noises she hears, of which there are many.

Ozzie has continued with her amazing talent of getting to places without us seeing her or escaping from Teddy and not being able to find her. Routines and accountability are essential when regularly stopping, unpacking and then starting another journey the following day.

So, before we drive off, I put Ozzie and Roo in their seats and then double check we have two dogs with us before we drive away. This is the most important part of the routine, closely followed by checking cupboards and lockers are closed, fridge on lock and running off the engine battery, gas switched off (very important), waste tank empty (where possible) and our fresh water full.

As with any routine we began with teething problems and had instances of being covered in pasta through forgetting to lock a cupboard. Early in the trip Roo was hit on the head by a box of phone chargers and as a result she won't sit anywhere near the guilty cupboard anymore. She looks at the cupboard when she walks past just in case by sheer chance something falls onto her again. I doubt she will forget this and will be cautious of this forever now.

So once everything is cabin checked we are ready for the off. I do my version of an inflight security check and make sure all passengers are aware of what to do in the event of an emergency! We pull away and I check behind to make sure the dogs are ok and amazingly see that Ozzie has jumped the barrier I use to keep them safe, and has managed to arrive in the front seat next to us whilst we drive. Despite our protests and thinly veiled warnings she continues to do this in the hope we either won't notice her or have changed our minds and want her next to us as we drive.

There have been countless occasions where she just vanishes. Paul and I constantly find ourselves checking where she is or calling her name trying to find her. She watches and waits until we are otherwise occupied and slips out of the door and then she is off.

One minute she is curled up on the front seat asleep and the next she is spotted at the window in the motorhome next to us or sniffing around the bins close by. This can get us into trouble and is also very embarrassing to be constantly walking around places shouting her name. We were alerted by an Austrian guy who found Ozzie in his motorhome looking longingly at his bed wanting to get in. She was also found by a German family they too were in a motorhome and found Ozzie trying desperately to get into one of the cupboards that had been left open. Ozzie was returned to us also by an elderly lady whilst in Switzerland. It was late and we were just about to retire for the night when she knocked on our door and had Ozzie in her arms asking if the dog was ours? My first thought was to say no as there was no way Ozzie could have disappeared she was under her blanket in the front seat right? Wrong! She had escaped again unnoticed and had spent a pleasant evening with this lady in her motorhome.

She has always been like this ever since we have had her. One occasion whilst in the UK and after spending hours and hours searching for her she was found by one of our neighbours who found her in his bed just as he pulled the sheets back to climb in. This gave him the fright of his life, his shock turning into relief for us all that she had eventually been found.

I had a lovely time and enjoyed the company of a lovely lady as I sat in her motorhome which was way nicer than ours. She fed me and gave me some tasty treats and then I curled up on the seat next to her for a hug. Some of the other people's motorhomes are not as friendly, especially one I visited which already had a dog. The food was just there on the floor in the bowl so of course I helped myself until I was rudely interrupted by a very loud voice but couldn't make head nor tail what he was saying so continued to devour the full contents of the bowl. I felt his hand underneath me as he picked me up and the next moment I found myself outside again. How rude I thought and he left me disorientated and I couldn't find Teddy. The bins were close by and this is where I tend to find the tastiest treats. As usual I just ignored the constant sound of my name being called and remained focused on the bin until I was unfortunately found by Emma and escorted back to our motorhome.

Most of the time Ozzie is wrapped tightly underneath/inside her blanket, just like a birthday present. Wrapping herself up like this is another of her talents and one that makes it harder for us to spot if she is still with us or has taken a fancy to a newer, larger motorhome.

Whenever I see Ozzie wrapped up tightly in her blanket it reminds me of when Roo got herself tangled in a single duvet quilt cover. I had bought the dogs quilts for the winter. The following morning I woke to find Roo in a state that can only be summarised as confused! During the night she had wriggled and managed to get herself in-between the plastic fastenings at the bottom of the quilt and when trying to get out got her head caught on one of the press studs. She look hilarious with this fastened to her as she tried to walk dragging the whole quilt with her.

Ozzie however has the ability to wrap herself up and get under her favourite blanket. We watch how she paws away at the blanket then lifts the corner with her mouth and then climbs underneath. She is such as talented dog really.

From Hamburg our next stop in Germany was Berlin and entailed us being dragged around a very busy city, and I can tell you that in this intense heat this was no fun! There was no breeze and I was struggling with the suffocating heat. Yes I do like the warmth on my back but this heat felt as though it was burning my skin. Emma always sprays us with lotion to protect our skin on hot days which I don't mind but today I felt as though I needed shade. After a while we stopped walking and soon forgot about the heat as I saw that someone had kindly left a disused barbeque, obviously for me as it still had the remains of grilled food attached to it which I instantly devoured.

Emma was more interested in standing Roo and I next to an old wall and taking our pictures, again. Seemingly this has something to do with the history of this place and used to run throughout this city. I stood still and behaved myself until the photographs were taken and then like a shot I raced off as my scent led me to yet another barbeque. This time loaded with burned meat, Roo and I feasted on this until the all too familiar clinking noise of the lead being attached around our collar and we got ushered away.

The blistering heat of the day was intense and the pavement was too hot for our paws to walk on. We had to stop walking as we couldn't walk any further and poor Roo was struggling with this too, her paws being far more sensitive than mine. As chance would have it our stop came at what turned out to be the world's longest beer festival and Paul was delighted. Can you believe we just stumbled across this? No neither could I but honestly we did! Luckily I found some shade and managed to get some water and cooled my paws off. I couldn't sleep as the noise and chaos going on around us meant I had to keep my wits about me. With all of the beer consumed by these people it was making them lose their balance and they became very wobbly, often wobbling into me and treading on my tail which I wasn't too pleased about.

We arrived in Berlin during a heatwave which made even the simplest of tasks become exhausting. Whilst the thought of constant sun and guaranteed heat is appealing to most people, this isn't ideal for those living in a tin box on wheels. The stellplatz was basic and crowded with little space between motorhomes yet this was to be expected and the location more than made up for this. It was in a district called Mitte and was an easy twenty minute walk into the centre of Berlin. Here we paid 20 euro per night and whilst this was more than double what we had paid so far, it was worth every penny for the opportunity to visit this great and historic city.

Our list of places to visit contained no real surprises. Checkpoint Charlie, the remains of the wall, Brandenburg gate and with one eye on exercising the dogs we added tiergarten with it being the largest and closest park.

With numerous options for visiting the remains of the wall we chose the East Side Gallery which is a very popular place for visitors. It runs for over a kilometre and has more than a hundred original art works by commissioned artists on it. This is the longest remaining segment of the Berlin Wall and despite visiting on a Saturday in the height of summer our tactic of visiting early in the morning ensure visitors were kept at a minimum.

From there we headed to Checkpoint Charlie and took photos of us, and the dogs in front of the Brandenburg gate. We had previously seen photos of the gate lit up at night so decided to return after nightfall for a different perspective.

Aware that the dogs needed to stretch their legs, tiergarten was thankfully a mere five minute walk and contained plenty of lakes for the dogs to cool off in. As city centre parks go, this was as good as it gets. Great walking routes and places we could let the dogs off, a zoo and lakeside bars.

By this stage the heat had taken its toll, we were all exhausted and despite cooling off in the lakes the dogs were starting to suffer. It was the hottest part of the day so we headed in the direction of the stellplatz and took refuge at an outdoor beer festival that was happening in the city centre. It turned out to be the world's longest beer festival, or beer garden. At over two kilometres long I doubt that anyone would get to sample all of the beers on offer, although some people were giving it a good go.

This place was sheer madness and as you would expect at a beer festival, was full of people of who were all enjoying the hundreds of different types of German beers on offer. We got chatting to a group of guys from Sweden who were on their way to getting drunk and they gave us their recommended for the best beers to sample. They spoke very good English though at times this was hard to make out as they constantly had their top lips bulging full with snuff that they regularly replenished. For those that aren't aware, snuff is a type of tobacco that you chew.

A couple of drinks later we realised it was still too hot and too busy a place for dogs so we agreed on a compromise. Head back to Teddy and Paul would return the next day on his own for a few hours. Decision made, we walked back to the stellplatz and relaxed for the night.

The following day was cooler and Paul headed off at midday for a few hours on his own whilst I relaxed with the dogs. He returned with a large smile on his face and a commemorative glass for me. Just what I've always wanted.

CHAPTER NINE

THE WALK

From Germany we headed east towards Poland which was filled with a mixture of emotions of highs and lows, plus a bucket load of education about the history of the country, none of which I ever remember being taught at school.

The first challenge we had was that we couldn't find any suitable camping or motorhome stops and so we looked at the cost of hotels and when we saw the price our only option was to book into a hotel. We were heading to Poznan for our first stop and found a hotel for 150 zloty a night which equates to 35 euro. It was situated within walking distance to Poznan town centre and I must admit I was looking forward to the luxuries of a hotel, hot running water, comfy bed and a flushing toilet. The things I used to take for granted. Checking into the hotel proved eventful as we realised we had no luggage bags to put our belongings in, plus we weren't 100% convinced they allowed dogs in their rooms.

When we booked online it claimed to be a dog friendly hotel and we did indicate we had dogs but this wasn't mentioned by the receptionist whilst we checked in so thought it best not to bring the subject up!

Luckily our room was on the ground floor and as luck would have it, our window was located exactly where Teddy was parked. We decided the most practical thing involved Paul emptying Teddy and handing to me our change of clothes, toiletries, dog food etc through the window and into the room. We even lifted the dogs through the window to save the trek of having to walk through the hotel, past the receptionist with the potential risk of being stopped and told to leave. You can imagine we got some strange looks from the other guests as they walked by.

We had never visited Poland and hadn't spoken to anyone who had visited this country before and our first impressions were surprisingly good. Especially the cost of food and drinks which were unbelievably cheap. Going out in the evening allowed us to enjoy drinks for well under a euro and a traditional meal consisting of dumplings, potatoes and cabbage cost around 1.50 euro.

A short walk from our hotel took us to Poznan town square. This was magnificent, with huge buildings surrounding it, all decorated with beautiful paintings which were very impressive and made this an outstanding backdrop to admire whilst soaking up the atmosphere. We spent a week in Poznan and had a few days just wandering around and learning about the Polish way of life, and the different foods and drinks that were on offer. Paul also went to a local football match whilst there, their team named Lech Poznan, where the fans have the tradition to turn their backs on the players, link arms and jump up and down each time they score! Predictably it finished 0-0 though he said the atmosphere was great.

I had heard Paul and Emma talking about our next destination and she didn't seem very keen on visiting. She had heard it was a bleak and a dull place with lots of poverty and unhappy people so I was surprised when I saw how beautiful and colourful Poland was. Poznan was our main stop here and we had the bonus of staying in a hotel. Though it was a strange hotel with presumably no front door as Roo and I entered and exited through the window. However, we had a great time and wandered around the old town and stopped off for snacks and drinks which was my favourite part. The dumplings and meat stew we had there were the best and we ate plenty of this, however I still had cravings for a bratwurst.

Our next stop in Poland was Krakow where we were lucky to find a campsite close enough to the city centre. Teddy's hot water boiler was still causing us problems as it only worked when it wanted to. We had been unable to get this fixed since our initial problems when we were in the UK which was over eight weeks ago. By this time we were growing tired with not knowing whether our showers would be hot or cold, so we knew something had to be done.

A Google search found a blog which then put us in touch with a local guy called Mike who visited us on the site, assessed the situation, and then directed us to his garage where we got a replacement boiler installed. This resulted in a large bill to include a new TV as we found that this was also broken when we bought the motorhome. This was yet another hidden cost we hadn't factored into our trip to add to the cost of the tyres we had to buy before leaving the UK.

Leaving Poznan, we headed south to Krakow and encountered one of the most boring days of our trip so far. Teddy had been naughty and was unable to turn the water hot so we had to take it to a garage to get fixed which took ages and we had to sit outside all day. We went on a couple of short walks but aside from that I slept most of the day. I constantly jumped up and pawed Emma to get her attention but she was busy talking. My cute face didn't even work this time.

Eventually after what took up most of the day Mike returned and told us the water boiler had been replaced and was now working. Seemingly the old one had been left with some water in the base of it during the winter and had frozen, which damages the elements.

We begrudgingly handed over the money for the new boiler and installation, though Mike did however transfer every episode from the TV series 24 onto a USB stick for us so we left with a working boiler, hot water and some TV to keep us entertained.

That evening I enjoyed the best shower ever, it was constantly hot, something we hadn't had in Teddy for weeks and I stayed in for the maximum time allowed, and I actually think I drained the whole tank of water. The shower in the motorhome is tiny and once you are in its difficult to move so you have to learn how to shower in the quickest time with minimal fuss. The drying process is also challenging due to the restrictions on space so this is far easier with the bathroom door open which isn't advisable when windows are open and you realise you've just flashed yourself to the whole campsite. You can imagine there's very little privacy living in a motorhome with windows all around you and neighbours within touching distance gawping in. It is surprising how quickly you adapt to situations and Paul and I are pretty good at the shower routine now and making sure we are covered and not on view.

When we bought Teddy it had been standing for some time unused and these are the types of things we didn't know about checking when we viewed it. Even now after spending eighteen months on the road we still learn every day about the mechanics and the way motorhomes work and also what can go wrong with them. As it's our house on wheels we try to look after it the best we can but travelling the distances we do there's always signs of wear and tear. On occasions we've had numerous bumps and scrapes and the most memorable was whilst driving on a motorway a large bird flew straight into us leaving a huge dent in the cabin above. Then we lost the lock to the side that keeps the gas locker secure, the back light fell off somewhere and then the gas cover also disappeared! Just like that, gone. With all the miles we do, the jostling about on roads, things just get loose and fall off. It is these types of things that can cause time and patience to find and replace as we know all motorhomes have different fittings. It always seems to happen just to us as most of the other motorhomes we see look like they have just been driven out of the showroom all immaculately clean and in pristine condition.

Poland so far had been good to us, the beauty of Poznan and Krakow combined with the luxury of now having hot water and a TV that works filled us with much excitement and these little things in life helped to gee us on to continue onto our next stop.

The next stage of our trip was a stop over and tour of Auschwitz which filled us with much sadness which wasn't surprising as it is just such an awful place. The free motorhome stop is actually in the car park of the old camp and on arrival you instantly sense a depressed heavy eerie feeling in the atmosphere.

Oddly though in the distance we heard music and walked in the general direction of the noise, intrigued to find where this was coming from. This took us to a large bar area amongst residential housing and there were literally hundreds of people there all dancing. All ages and all shapes and sizes. It was 5pm on a Friday night and it was a welcome sight after the depressing vibes we had felt only minutes earlier at the camping park. Though it was also an odd sight and one that I haven't quite unraveled in my mind.

The next morning we were up early to walk the dogs before heading into the camp. I watched as both dogs retreated as we walked past this ghastly place. They do say that dogs have a sixth sense and this was extremely evident here. Their behaviour was unsettled and they were keen to get back to the motorhome not wanting to spend much of their time outdoors which is the opposite of what they are usually like. We also noticed no wildlife in the area and no birds at all which they say never fly over the camp.

Auschwitz can only be described as hell on earth, the torture and suffering that was carried out there was just appalling and I couldn't continue the full tour. My anger and hatred for those who carried out the unearthly torturing, not wanting to walk on the same ground that these evil people once had.

I wanted to go and found the whole experience extremely upsetting and I was so pleased to get back to Teddy to see Ozzie and Roo. That night we lit a candle in respect and to remember the estimated 1.1 million prisoners who died there. Writing this piece and reflecting back on this tour still brings me to tears and is a place I will always remember but leaves a real sense of sadness and despair.

I wanted to add a piece here in dedication to Anne Frank as following my tour of Auschwitz I read her diaries and was so gripped by her words, her skill and her ability to write her amazing story. I showed my respect to her when we visited her grave in Bergen Belsen and I have no words to describe the sorrow I have for her. She truly was an amazing person and I find it ironic to see this quote of hers.

"I keep my ideals, because in spite of everything I still believe that people are really good at heart". Anne Frank: 1929 – 1945

We went to this weird place that I sensed was sad and had an awful smell and feeling about it. We approached the gates and a small sign said (no dogs allowed) which I was pleased about as my gut instinct told me that I didn't want to enter the building. I looked up and there were no birds in the air. For miles and miles of sky there was nothing. Very weird.

Roo and I both stayed in Teddy and gazed out of the window and waited for their return and I could see Emma approaching us and saw she was upset and she was crying. Of all the places we have visited so far this is the worst and I don't ever want to go back there. It felt sad and depressing and Roo and I were quite happy staying indoors. It filled me with relief when I heard

Paul start the engine and we moved off, thank goodness and please do not bring me back here.

The four of us were in much need of being cheered up and left the camp ground in Auschwitz and headed out of Poland with plans to stop in Slovakia and then onto Austria.

We travelled briefly through Slovakia as we only stayed for one night. After driving for hours looking for a place to stay this proved unsuccessful and our only option was to spend the night in a hotel car park and this was only agreed after I pleaded with the receptionist to allow us to stay there. Our impressions are that this country is not motorhome friendly and we found no facilities nor sites to stop at whilst there.

Whilst there we did find a friendly bar and they allowed us charge our mobile phones and ordered us a takeaway pizza which was a real treat. No cooking and no dishes. We were settled and felt safe in the car park for the night but later that evening we were woken by the thunderous sound of an almighty storm that shook us from side to side. Rain leaked in through all of the cracks and seals making it an unsettled night and having to comfort the dogs, mop up the rain water and contend with the almighty racket from the thunder storm.

The following morning was bright with blue skies and unbelievably there was no evidence nor sign of any damage from the storm. Opening the side door to let some sunshine in, Ozzie spotted a dog and its owner walking in the far distance. This is when she darted out and raced at them, barking and howling furiously. This made them turn and run away in the opposite direction followed by me running behind to catch Ozzie.

I caught up with her just as the owner let go of her dogs lead and both Ozzie and her dog greeted each other with a bottom sniff and then had a wild time chasing each other playing as friends. I was exhausted chasing Ozzie and the owner of the other dog was clearly furious with Ozzie's approach as her excitement to greet them had startled her. I apologised and she let rip shouting and I think swearing at in a Slovakian dialect. Although alarmed I did realise that Ozzie was out of order and I don't know what had made her see red. I apologised and quickly made my exit as she was still cursing at me and as I turned to leave she gave me a hand gesture to show what she really thought of me and my naughty Beagle.

All I had done was get out to stretch my legs when I saw the dog ahead of me. I sprinted to catch the scent of the dog. I really just wanted to play with it but guess I got carried away and little too excited. There was a one sided argument which I think it may have had something to do with me but I wasn't entirely sure as the other lady was screaming and shouting at Emma. I got ushered back to Teddy and Emma didn't speak to me. Even when I jumped up to her and tried to get a treat from her pocket she pushed me away. I hate it when she falls out with me but this only usually lasts a few hours.

Leaving Slovakia was eventful to say the least. We had parked on a grass verge to let the dogs out for a pee as by now Ozzie was bursting. Within minutes three young men got out of a car nearby, approached us and told us to move. With no explanation given, just to move. Of course we did as we were told and didn't ask any questions.

Foot down on the accelerator and some wheel spins later we crossed the border leaving Slovakia and into Austria. This was country number seven of our trip and a place we had been looking forward to since Mike, our mechanic and TV supplier in Poland, had waxed lyrical about its beauty.

Our first stop was spent at a vineyard called Sloboda near a lake in Podersdorf Am See where motorhomes can stay on the grounds with all facilities for only 10 euro a night or this fee is waived if you buy twelve bottles of their wine. The vineyard was small and had a bar area around ten metres from where the motorhomes park up and was a fantastic place to spend a few days. There were endless walks through the many vines in the area and along the lake side and is memorable for having the best walking we had experienced up to this point of our trip.

Whilst walking in the area we were alarmed by the ongoing sound of gun fire that let out an almighty boom sporadically or more so as you approached the vines. This was especially worrying as the dogs were off their leads and the booms seemed to be coming from wherever they ran. We spoke to a worker who was picking grapes from the vines who explained that the vines have sensors and speakers on them that are triggered by anyone, or anything that gets close to them and give off a loud gun fire sound to deter unwanted visitors. This made us feel safer and we understood they were targeted at the birds in the area, preventing them from eating the merchandise.

From here we headed to Vienna for a couple of nights where I picked up some mail from the poste restante there. A very important delivery this was, numerous fashion and make up magazines kindly posted to me from my friend Gillian in the UK. This was surely worth the traffic jams, difficulties in finding a parking place big enough for a motorhome and a 40 kilometre detour, not to mention the challenge of finding the delivery office in the large city. Its things like this that I really missed from home as I always like to keep up to date with the current trends so I was happy and surely that's the main thing!

We stayed for a couple of nights near another vineyard located right near the Danube (Donau) river. The second longest river in Europe no less. More dog walks, more delicious wine and some great conversations with the locals that led us to think that this is a country that we will one day revisit as we certainly didn't see everything there.

Driving south from Austria and into Slovenia we arrived in Maribor in under four hours which included a stop off for us all to use the toilet. Maribor is the largest ski resort in Slovenia during the winter months and was fairly quiet during summer when we were there. We were just going to pass through this country but were pleasantly surprised as we drove through as the landscape was pretty so decided to stop off for a few days. We followed our camper contact app to a campsite and on arrival we found it well equipped and fairly cheap, clean and we soon got Teddy parked up, plugged into the electric point, filled our water tank and emptied our waste.

Throughout our trip we usually tended to stay away from commercial campsites as they are generally more expensive than motorhome stops and are usually better suited to families, with additional facilities such as swimming pools, restaurants and entertainment that we don't use.

The resources we use to find motorhome accommodation are a combination of the camper contact app, internet and general recommendations from other motorhomers. Generally our criteria is to look for a clean place with Wi-Fi, good dog walking/running, electric hook up and bathroom, in that order of importance, having a laundry is an additional bonus though I tended to do hand washing on the go.

On arrival to a stop for the night we have developed a routine where we both have our own roles and duties. Paul usually drives Teddy into the site, and I get out of the passenger seat and look around before directing him into a spot that looks good and large enough to fit Teddy.

We have named this stage of our routine, 'The Walk' and find that most motorhomers, regardless of age, nationality or wealth do the same thing. 'The Walk' always makes us laugh as it reminds us of a pallbearer and their duty to guide a hearse but of course this is in a completely different context.

Once happy and in a spot for the night, Paul makes sure we are level and we do the egg test. This is where an egg is placed on the table in the motorhome and if it rolls we need the levellers out. If it remains still, we don't need them and we can rest assured we are straight and level. A very scientific test we think and if we run out of eggs, then apples, oranges or potatoes do the same job.

Paul then untangles the electric cable (the one that had no tangles or knots that same morning) and plugs this into the mains. My job is to get the outdoor furniture ready, tidy up inside clearing up what has dropped or spilt during the journey and then open all of the air vents and windows to let the air in. However, some of these window hatches have snapped, so we use wooden spoons and spatulas to perform this operation. I then open the outside awning and depending on the time of day make us all some food or snacks to eat whilst we get used to our surroundings.

This whole routine may seem lengthy and onerous but it only takes us about 5 minutes to get settled. We watch other motorhomes arrive and the passenger gets out (usually the woman) and performs "The Walk" and then carries out their own similar routine with some people taking hours to get settled only to then move off again within a few minutes whereas others have it perfected and are parked up and have made this place their home within seconds.

People watching is one of my favourite pastimes. One of the best moments was when we watched a couple arrive and parked up and then drove forward for one inch and then reversing back an inch. They would get settled and plugged in with electricity before deciding that an inch really does make a difference and start the engine again to drive and reverse the motorhome an inch forward and backwards again. As if trying to rock their motorhome to sleep. This went on for well over an hour and I was close to going over and helping them as they were driving me mad, firing the engine up every five minutes. They must surely have realised that each time they decided they had reached the correct position, it was in exactly the same place it was previously. This left us confused as to why they were doing this and to this day still haven't worked it out.

I need to explain here about the names of the camping spots as they differ depending on what country you are. So in France they are called Aires, Germany they are Stellplatz and elsewhere they are camping or parking areas. Some people drive into an aire/stellplatz/ camping area with the sole goal of trying to get the best spot for satellite television. These motorhomes are usually, (correction always) French. We watched a French motorhome in Holland drive round and round the camping spot for hours to try and get a picture on their TV. They were even conducting surveys of those already on the site to work out location, direction and probably wind speed. Watching French TV must really be worthwhile and is on my list of things I must do.

Back in Slovenia and Paul and I were sitting outside finishing lunch and planning a walk which would take us up to Mount Pohorje. The cable cars operate in the summer months for the benefit of hikers and mountain bikers so we decided to walk up and catch one to get us back down.

We were getting our backpacks ready for our trek when a small girl appeared at our door with her brother and asked in a very polite English voice "can we walk your dogs?" They were a family from Guernsey who were parked just across from us. I was happy as we were several weeks into our trip and aside from Paul, had not had a conversation with an English person since leaving the UK. Yes I had called home a few times and spoken to friends and family but this was to be my first face to face English conversation in a long while.

They were a lovely family who had decided to travel Europe in their motorhome for ten months and then return in September for the children to begin school. They were a real inspiration and lovely to meet and they also gave us lots of hints and tips of places we could visit as they had already been on the road for six months. They informed us that there had been a Champions League game the night before between NK Maribor and Celtic FC and I could sense Paul kicking himself as he would have loved to have experienced that, if only we had arrived a day earlier he would have been able to go.

After finding out about their travels Paul and I headed off for our walk, the heat was quite intense but we had packed water, some lunch and a bag of twiglets to keep us going. The mountain was a hive of activity with bikers zooming down on mountain bikes and some people Nordic walking winding in-between the wooded areas.

Paul and I headed straight up the middle track of the mountain. This part was the steepest but was also the clearest and we wanted to keep the dogs in our sight and away from the bikers. For once the dogs obeyed our commands, they raced off as they usually do, though this time they came back when we called. We watched Ozzie as she ran through the long grass racing off into the distance, her legs kicking straight behind her. She was howling with ecstasy and running around as if she were a puppy, charging in-between our legs then off up the mountain she went. This made us smile, she was happy and loving her time here and we both commented that she looked like she was actually enjoying herself. Hopefully feeling happy and ridding herself of the awful anxiety she had suffered in the past after losing Miffy.

This is what I wanted and needed in my life, I loved this place and the smells here drove me crazy. There is just so much freedom and space here and Roo kept up with me and enjoyed her freedom too. I know that I hadn't been feeling as anxious as I usually do and I was sleeping better without any nasty dreams and this can only be due to the fact that I am happier and more content with myself. Yes I still think about Miffy and miss her dearly but she would be proud of me I'm sure. Look at what I've achieved so far and I'm only 6 years old. There is no way I'm turning to dust, not for a long time yet anyway.

Roo and I continued running up the mountain and we were loving being released from our leads. We raced through the woods, my nose to the ground sniffing all of the delicious smells just sent me wild. I ran and ran and my ears flapped in the wind and I yelped loudly to get Roo's attention to let her know where I was. I heard my name being called several times and for some reason I behaved and stayed within sight of Paul and Emma but only because I knew they had twiglets that I ended up eating for them.

My legs were aching when we all eventually stopped at the top of the large mountain. Despite the sun it was cold at the top and Paul picked me up to warm me and gave me a cuddle as I had been good on this walk and hadn't rolled in any poo, honest! As I sat in Paul's arms we both looked out across the vista. He squeezed me tightly as he always does which makes me feel safe and he kissed me on the nose, he is still my favourite person.

Once at the top of the mountain Paul and I were boiling hot, it was a really warm day and the sky was a beautiful dark blue colour which looked amazing against the backdrop of Maribor town centre in the distance. It had taken us about three hours to climb which is quite an achievement considering the warm weather conditions but being on the top and eating our sandwiches it soon became cloudy and cold. We put our fleece jackets on and headed to the cable car for a quick descent as we didn't want to hang around for too long due to the change in climate. This was Ozzie and Roo's first trip in a cable car and they were loving it. Well Ozzie was, Roo fell asleep as soon as it started to move off.

After my hug I wriggled to the ground and I was off again. It was a long way up so I knew it was the same down and I was raring to go but I noticed Paul and Emma had started heading in the opposite direction. They were walking up some steps so I raced and followed them got crammed into a small red box thing that I noticed was just dangling from the sky by a very thin line.

It was great that we had the carriage to ourselves and Ozzie sat next to us on the seat and watched out of the window as we went down. I guess we are lucky to have such adaptable dogs and they have experienced so much since embarking on the trip from ferries, lifts, escalators and now cable cars.

We sat in this thing for a minute or two and I looked out of the window just as we started to move. It was great and I could see for miles. I sat on the seat, upright so I could look out and I saw the other hounds running around underneath me. I barked for them to hear me but they couldn't as the glass surrounding us was thick and we were very high up which felt strange. Roo wasn't as impressed as I was with this mode of transport and fell asleep on the floor next to us not bothered or appreciating our first trip in what I now know to be a cable car.

It eventually stopped and we all headed out into the warm air again, Roo feeling refreshed after her power nap. I felt good, my legs ached now and my stomach was empty and I knew that Roo was feeling the same and wanted food. Roo is a great sister and companion and tells me exactly when it is time for us to be fed. Once she has decided it is time for food, either breakfast or dinner as we get fed twice daily, she pesters Emma by pawing at her legs and jumping at her. Although we were both hungry I knew this walk wasn't over just yet as Teddy was still a distance away so by the time we got back Roo and I were ravenous.

The next few days flew past in a blur. We did nothing more than relax and walk the dogs into the woods around the mountain.

Croatia was next on our list and we initially planned on making the journey in one trip and arriving just after lunch the next day. A chance conversation with another couple made us rethink this plan. They had only just arrived in Maribor having spent 10 hours stuck at the border to get out of Croatia. Being the height of summer and a weekend clearly wasn't the best time to enter Croatia.

Our route remained largely the same, with an overnight stop just past Ljubljana added, leaving us with a much shorter drive to the border on Monday morning. We paid over 30 euro for the privilege of staying on this average site and with a reluctance to spend any more money in their bar or restaurant we walked the dogs in our first rain for some time and retreated to Teddy for a cosy night ready for an early start.

Miffy and Ozzie once they have bonded

My Favourite Person

Ozzie and Roo at Berlin Wall

Paul and Ozzie in Pompeii

Ozzie, Roo and Emma on the beach in Palamos

Ozzie and Teddy in Croatia

Paul and Ozzie in Teddy

New Year's Eve in Seville (with fireworks)

Ozzie in Norway

Ozzie in Chamonix

CHAPTER TEN

DANGLY BITS IN CROATIA

Despite arriving at the border in Croatia early in the morning to miss the crowds we still encountered what was our first real traffic jam of our trip. As well as a volume of cars and single track roads they do seem to carry out more stringent checks of motor vehicles passing through this particular border. It may possibly be due to only recently joining the EU, however if you do travel to Croatia please bear this in mind as you could be stuck here for hours if you arrive at the wrong time of day.

Once we had crossed the border the signs for campsites were clearly marked out and as we drove across the cliff tops we could see the crystal blue sea in the distance which looked very inviting. We came across a camping area which was literally 50 yards from the sea, overlooking the beach and near a small village called Umag where we parked up for the night.

On entering the site I did 'the walk', and once our routine to get Teddy organised was completed we picked up our beach bag, threw in some drinking water and headed straight towards the beach. The sea was an amazing turquoise colour glinting in the sun. So perfect in fact that it looked more like an infinity swimming pool that you see at luxury resorts. You could even see small fish swimming in the shallow parts and the water was warm, just like stepping into a bath.

Paul and I dived in closely followed by Roo whilst Ozzie observed us from the shore not even getting her paws wet. This gave Roo the opportunity to show us her new trick where she dives underwater fully submerged and retrieves pebbles from the bed below. This trick of hers has attracted a lot of attention and passersby who often stopped to watch and take pictures of her. She just loves the attention and will retrieve the exact same pebble that's thrown in for her. Whilst doing this a crowd of people congregated as she repeatedly dived in the water and retrieved pebbles. Like a celebrity she was filmed and photographed by the hordes of tourist paparazzi keen to get the best shot. We are now used to her drawing in the crowds now and no doubt she is on numerous cameras and photographs all over the world.

We were enjoying the luxury of the warm sea and the heat of the sun dried us in no time as we wandered along the beach towards a small beach bar. Actually it claimed to be a beach club and the dogs had never been to a beach club before so this was a first. On our approach towards the bar we noticed we were surrounded by lots of naked people. Lots and lots of naked people, in fact there were hundreds of them! They were all elderly, and some had propped themselves up on their walking frames and others had found a comfortable spot on beach mats and lilos. In the distance we noticed more naked people getting out of their cars with beach bags, all in their birthday suits with not a stitch on! Everyone was completely naked, well apart from us that is.

As I was running along the beach to catch up with Paul and Emma I could see lots of people not too far away and they all look odd though I couldn't put my paw on what it was that made them stand out to be different.

I then realise that all of these people did not have any clothes on! All of them, no clothes, they were all naked! Now that I had noticed this I couldn't stop staring. Looking more closely and saw they had wrinkles on their bodies from head to toe. I didn't even know you could get wrinkles where these people had wrinkles! Some of the ladies breasts were hanging very low and they reminded me of Bella my friend from home, she is a spaniel and has very long droopy ears just like the ladies breasts.

I also noticed that the men amongst them had dangly bits and some of these were dangling dangerously low. This fascinated me and I watched these people for some time and wondered why they were all there. All without their clothes on.

This was my first dog walk in Croatia and I was curious about these people, who they were, and why they were not wearing any clothes. Maybe this was the thing to do here. Personally I always like to keep myself well covered and wouldn't dream of leaving the house without my collar on.

The sun was drying us out as we continued our walk along the beach past the group of sunbathers who had turned the beach next to us into a nudist colony. Feeling slightly over dressed in flip flops, shorts and a t-shirt and trying not to stare, which is easier said than done, we held our heads high and wandered in between them towards the beach bar. Despite us being the only people favouring clothes in this part of Croatia they didn't seem to notice us, even when Ozzie ran straight up to one gentleman and gave him a sniff in a very personal area which he didn't seem to mind, he simply glanced down at her and gently shooed her away.

We took refuge in the beach club and reflected that nudity in this area must just be viewed as a normal occurrence. For a split second we considered joining them, then we remembered we are British and declined the opportunity to show our bare bodies. Plus my regular preen was overdue and I didn't want to scare the locals.

Living in a motorhome can have limitations of keeping trim and the beauty regime nowadays had long gone out of the window.

As I say, the majority of the nudists were elderly, retired, or of retirement age. The wrinklies as we now call them were everywhere. Like buses, once you see one another comes along, then another, and all you could see all along the beach front was a sea of nakedness all in different colours, shapes and sizes.

One gentleman stuck out like a sore thumb. (Pardon the pun) He was the only one out of them all that was very tall at well over 6ft and had decided to match his birthday suit, with a pair of brilliant white, knee high socks. Very fetching I had to admit and his demeanor was one of a carefree attitude, a belief that he looked irresistible as he sprawled himself out on his hessian beach mat soaking up the rays. I wondered why he would choose to just wear socks and arrived at the conclusion that he must have really ugly feet.

Very quickly you just got used to seeing lots and lots of naked old people and after a while you didn't take a second look. They were all enjoying their day, chatting to one another perfectly relaxed and enjoying themselves which in fact was lovely to see.

It was now lunchtime and we decided to park the beach club for the moment as we were getting a little peckish and so started to head back to Teddy for a barbeque. As we approached the camping spot where we were parked up, we heard the sound of dogs barking and as we turned saw six tiny white fluffy dogs racing towards us.

At first we just ignored their yelps and continued our walk but they soon caught up with us and started to nip Roo's ankles trying to encourage her to play. Ozzie wasn't having any of it and darted off in the opposite direction away from them and leaving poor Roo to fend them off herself. Although they were tiny they were very vocal yappy dogs and were making a hell of a racket. In the distance we saw a woman come running towards us who we guessed was the owner of these little devils. Roo by this time was yelping and standing on them as she tried to dodge their nips but this just made them even more persistent and they continued to annoy her even more.

The woman came from the direction of the nudist colony and as she approached us we saw she had a small white towel wrapped around herself. She was shouting at the dogs as she came running towards us and looked annoyed that they had ran off. We tried to catch the dogs for her but they chased and darted away making it impossible to stop or catch them. They were like fluffy balls of candy floss blowing in the wind and they raced in between our legs and were so small and very fast you couldn't catch them. Each one had a good set of teeth which they would happily bare and show us when we tried to stop them.

The woman had their leads and managed to catch two of them straight away leaving the other four dogs to run off. The two dogs pulled like mad on the leads which forced her arm making her towel drop to the floor and yes she was naked, but was clearly not part of the wrinkly brigade. She looked in her early 30's with a pretty face and blonde long hair. The dropping of the towel didn't bother her at all as she was in no rush to pick it up or cover herself. Fair play I thought to myself, if I had a body like hers I would be happy to wander around naked all day. She continued to chase the remaining four stray dogs before turning back to us to apologise at the same time as picking up her towel as she headed back towards the dogs by which time were on the beach. I willed Paul to erase this beauty before him from his mind and to stick to reality of what he has, ie me. On a positive note though, I am thankful that my dangly bits don't dangle yet and thankfully still have a few firm years ahead of me yet!

We had arrived back at Teddy and due to the heat I was wishing for the doors to open as I was so hot and needed some water. I could feel sweat beads running down my oversized nose and onto my whiskers. Roo was sitting way too close to me which was making me feel even hotter. I tried to gently nudge her out of the way to get some room but she ignored me and on occasions such as these I had to remind her who is boss.

I deal with Roo in an authoritative way and I have to warn her to stay away from the water dish until I have had a drink. The rules, I have decided, are that no matter how thirsty Roo is, she must wait until I have had a drink first. This is now called 'Ozzies law' and whilst it wouldn't stand up in a court of doggy law it goes for all drinking even when we are outside, so includes lakes, streams and even puddles. Roo does however sometimes try to sneak to the bowl and sip a drink but I always spot her and race to knock her out of the way because I always have to drink first.

I really did need a drink and saw the water bowl glistening straight ahead of me which I literally dived into. After drinking most of the water in the bowl in one visit I realised I was still incredibly hot. Outside it was even hotter and luckily I found some shade underneath Teddy. I had to take a deep breath to fit under Teddy and squatted my legs low to get right underneath and headed to the coolest spot. My stomach flat on the cool ground and I lay there sprawled out cooling my body from the heat.

Mid doze I was aware that Roo kept bothering me and returned back to check on me time and time again and after entertaining the people on the beach with her diving skills she too was tired and was desperately trying to fit her long gangly body underneath Teddy to be with me but after several attempts she gave up. She is much bigger than me and there was no way she could fit.

That afternoon I slept and had some happy dreams, my eyes opened and I was relieved as I felt that it was much cooler being later in the day. I breathed in and managed to wriggle out from under Teddy and was instantly furious to see Paul, Emma and Roo all sitting together eating food without me.

I was so annoyed that they didn't wake and include me and charged towards them and straight into Emma who was the closest to the food. She threw me a small piece of cheese which she does occasionally to keep me happy and to stop me pestering her and I have learnt that she does this more often if I put my cute face on. My cute face consists of simultaneously raising my eyes, tilting my head and pricking up one of my ears. It has taken years to perfect this and now works every time.

The following days brought us more blue skies and hot sunshine and these days were becoming part of the norm now and we found that Roo and I didn't have the energy to walk, never mind run.

With Emma always being full of energy I wasn't surprised that we were always taken on our usual early morning run but for the first time in my memory my legs felt as if they were not mine and I lagged behind and just couldn't catch up. I was physically zapped and slowly limped back to Teddy and lay underneath where I spent most of my days. I didn't get to see too much of Croatia because of the heat but learnt a lot about the engineering and mechanics of what goes on underneath our motorhome.

Continuing our journey Paul drove, whilst I checked the map for our next stop. We passed Pula and decided against catching a ferry to one of the small islands off the coast of Croatia and instead headed to Draga. We found the campsites in this area expensive in comparison to the other sites we had stopped at in Europe so we followed a motorhome sign and ended up in the garden of someone's house. This was a privately owned business to allow motorhomers to park up and plug into their electricity points. The price was 25 euro for the night, not cheap, but a lot cheaper than the campsites.

Draga was a typical holiday resort scattered with small kiosks selling souvenirs and a few beach front restaurants. Signs pointed out that the beach doesn't allow dogs though further signposts pointed along the beach to a dog friendly zone. Blink and I guarantee you will miss this. I am not exaggerating to say it was the size of a postage stamp! It was tiny and set slightly up on rocks with no access to the sea. I've racked my brains without success trying to think of what breed of dog could get sufficient exercise in this space but I do know that Ozzie and Roo were not impressed. The intense heat however ensured that exercise of any substance wasn't required and we spent a pleasant evening in Teddy swatting mosquitos and making the most of the electricity we had to charge laptops and mobiles phones.

Senj was our next stop and was a place I would definitely recommend. A designated car park for motorhomes literally right on the sea front. It was fairly full, though there was more than enough space between the motorhomes. At 7 euro per night this was more like it. We stayed for three nights and really enjoyed the feel of this town.

Decent looking restaurants, bars and walks meant it ticked most of our boxes. The only negative here was when a local lady frantically and quite vocally objected to Ozzie using the pavement to pee on. A discussion followed where I questioned how I was supposed to control the movement of water from Ozzie. Aside from making her wear a nappy I am still clueless as to the problem here. Any responsible dog owner carries bags and takes responsibility to ensure that number twos are picked up. As for wees I'm yet to see any dog owner, anywhere, come up with a solution to stop dogs peeing wherever they like.

Our time in Senj was spent weighing up options to either head further south and catch a ferry from Split into Ancona in Italy, or head north and across the border to head for Venice. We couldn't make a decision so it was a relief to learn that the ferries weren't running to Italy at this time of year. Whether this information was correct is questionable but our decision was made.

We had also been getting really concerned with the heat and how it was affecting the dogs as every day temperatures soared well over the thirty degree mark with Ozzie spending most of her days underneath the motorhome to keep cool.

Decision made, we started our journey back to the border and because of the previous traffic jams and delays of getting through the border and into Croatia we planned to cross early Monday morning which we guessed would be a quieter time. We started the ascent northwards on the Sunday and thankfully the roads were quiet, the scenery was beautiful and the landscape really breathtaking and as we drove we spotted a bay that looked amazing. Set in between mountains and the inlet of the sea looked like a lake, and a little piece of heaven.

I noticed another motorhome parked up and I asked if they were staying the night as this looked like a great spot to spend an evening. They were from Switzerland and looked in their late 70's and spoke very little English so communicated with a mime with my hands clasped eyes shut pretending I was asleep and then pointing to the motorhome and giving the thumbs up, she responded with a nod and a thumbs up back. I took this as a yes and felt happier that we didn't have to keep driving as the heat was way too much for the dogs to cope with.

Our day was spent chilling out and popping in and out of the sea to cool off and before dinner we all went for a run in the mountains, as the sun was setting, there was a cool breeze and the dogs looked relieved. Ozzie and Roo raced ahead of us as they usually do to chase each other, always full of energy after relaxing all day, which is always good to see.

We ran for miles over the hills and followed the coastal path that lead us to a small village called Bakar and on our return to Teddy we dived in the clear crystal blue waters and afterwards hung our clothes out to dry on the cycle rack on the back of the motorhome.

After we had freshened up and had some food we headed to the local tavern for a drink. It was only a five minute walk away from where we were parked and it also had Wi-Fi which is always a bonus.

The table at the front was available and we took the seats there overlooking the sea and then gave our order to the waitress. I will always remember this waitress as her shoes had springs on them where the heel bit usually is. This made her walk with a spring in her step and she was springing all over the place. She was very amusing to watch as she sprang in and out of the bar getting orders from the customers, springing to get the drinks and springing backwards and forwards. It was obvious that she was popular with the male clientele in the bar due to the fact that her springs made her wobble and it was evident she didn't own a sports bra which in my opinion was warranted.

The drinks were brought to us by springy (my new name for her) and were lovely, cold and refreshing. So nice in fact, that we drank them in no time at all. Whilst sitting and soaking up the views I noticed a man sitting at the table next to us who was trying to catch our attention. I turned to smile and say hello and his one word back to me was "motorhome!" I smiled back and acknowledged "yes motorhome".

He responded, "I have house, you stay?" My reply was, "thank you" but "no thank you". I stopped the eye contact after this very brief exchange of words as I had an inclination that he, or the situation was a bit weird.

Unfortunately he moved seats, right in front of us and said "Beagle?" Ozzie was sitting next to me and her ears pricked up! Patting her on the head to reassure her I replied "yes Beagle". His eyes lit up and at first I was pleased that at last someone likes Ozzie as it is always Roo that gets the attention and compliments. Maybe he isn't weird and just a dog lover. I was wrong!

His next words were, "I take Beagle and hunt in the woods for hog?" After a brief discussion it transpired that basically he wanted to take Ozzie from us and keep her to go hunting for wild boar in the woods. He claimed that there were plenty of hogs roaming this area at this time of year! This conversation has to be one of the weirdest I have had in my life as he failed to understand why I wouldn't give up my dog to him. He had money to make and he was adamant Ozzie could help him make this and sniff out these hogs.

I have no doubt Ozzie would be a champion hog sniffer as she has the nose of a Beagle and can sniff out anything, but she wasn't going anywhere.

Eventually after much explaining and miming out scenes to him as he only spoke a little English and I don't speak Croatian he started to understand that he couldn't have her and that she is part of our family. He seemed to understand this, though then replied "motorhome, you have motorhome?" followed by "I have house you stay there?"

I was getting tired with this conversation now so deviated past him to springy and ordered some more drinks and a change of seat to get away from hog man which I now called him.

The sun was going down, the scenery was beautiful, we were happy and content and the hog man had left so no more hassle about taking Ozzie from us. We left the bar, as we saw hog man reappear so we finished our drinks and made an extra quick exit back to the safety of Teddy noticing the Swiss motorhome that had been parked next to us earlier had left, meaning we were alone!

I was very relieved to be back in Teddy and glanced at Roo, she too looked worried. We both know that I was worried that Emma would have given me to that man and then I would have to go and live with him and spend my time hunting for hogs. There was one point where I thought I was going, so I made sure I was sitting as close as I could to Emma, putting my cute face on. I'm pretty sure that Paul would never let me go but I found being in this situation difficult and I couldn't fully relax and yes my anxiety had reappeared.

That night I lay awake just looking out of the window and I could see a huge cloud moving towards us and it looked angry. The air felt like it was closing in and I sensed a storm was brewing. My stomach was one gigantic knot and all of my senses were alert. Roo lay fast asleep next to me and I knew it would take some storm to wake her up. Unless she has an inkling that there may be some food imminently served up she can literally sleep through anything, unlike me.

My senses were right about the storm and inevitably the flashes of lightening started, followed by huge crashes of thunder. The storm was directly above us and my anxiety heightened at a rate that made me vomit, luckily away from where I was sitting, and still Roo didn't wake up. She never minds when I'm sick anyway, she likes it, as it means she gets to eat it up for me.

I couldn't stop trembling and my paws and whole body were shaking. The wind from the storm was making the motorhome rock from side to side and the waves from what was previously the calm sea were crashing over us. I shut my eyes as tightly as I could hoping it would just go away but it didn't.

Paul and I had only been asleep for a short while before we were woken by a horrendous storm and we were literally in the eye of it unable to move and with no apparent escape from it. This place had been such a peaceful spot through the day and indeed was still calm around an hour ago. Now it was looking and feeling more like a war zone. Looking out of the window the flashes of lightning were constant and the waves were actually crashing against the motorhome at times completely engulfing us. This continued for a good couple of hours with the powerful winds and rain shaking us around like a paper bag which made us feel incredibly isolated, helpless and vulnerable.

I found poor Ozzie a quivering wreck shaking profusely and her eyes tightly shut as she sat on her usual seat. She had also been sick and I could see this was really stressing her out. Roo of course was curled up next to her snoozing and wasn't fretting about the commotion that was happening outside.

I comforted Ozzie and cuddled her tightly and prayed that the storm would pass soon but deep down I knew it was getting worse. The storm was now literally on top of us and at one point I thought we would end up in the sea. Despite the severity of the situation I remembered we had hung our clothes up on the cycle rack at the back of the motorhome after our run. I knew that by now they would have been blown away and I cursed myself for leaving my new trainers outside along with Paul's favourite pair of running shorts.

I didn't want to be a sitting duck by staying here, but there was no way I was going outside to check if it was as bad as it sounded. I started to panic which meant Ozzie and I were both now comforting each other and no use to anyone. There was one point that I thought we were going to die and this is when I became hysterical and urged Paul to move us.

Paul by this time was now fully awake and contemplating our options in his own laid back manner. Whilst doing this he had to contend with calming me down and also dealing with Ozzie's anxieties a real challenge! It was wild outside and was in pitch darkness which made it all more disorientating. No lights from the street and no stars or moon to provide a glimpse of visibility just total darkness. All we had was noise. After narrowing our options down to one choice we agreed we should move and go somewhere sheltered and safer.

That night when the storm erupted I was willing Paul to take us away from this place. First of all I was nearly taken away from my family to go and hunt hogs and now I was potentially going to perish in the storm. Roo eventually woke up and looked startled to see that we were all awake and active and immediately rushed to devour the pile of sick that I had brought up.

Paul is so laid back which is a godsend at times like this. A level head is what is needed and I could sense him wondering what the panic was about as he casually got into the driver seat, started the engine and we drove off away from the dreadful storm.

Within a matter of minutes it turned calmer and more settled. In a layby we pulled over and checked the motorhome for any damage of which thankfully there was none. The only thing damaged was our broken sleep, and some missing running gear. We decided it would be best to get further away from the storm and we continued to drive looking for a spot to pull into that looked safe. It was by this time 4am in the morning and the roads were quiet and we were all very tired and needed some sleep.

In the distance we saw one of the most recognizable signs in the world, a large golden M which we headed for, only to find that it wasn't a 24 hour place and closed but the car park was open and empty. We pulled into a space, shut the blinds and within seconds were all fast asleep and the troubles of the last few hours were well and truly forgotten.

When travelling it is like riding a rollercoaster, lows, quickly replaced by massive highs and thankfully there are far more highs than lows.

At 7am we all woke, feeling slightly jetlagged and Paul and I popped into the café for a breakfast and coffee. Treating Ozzie and Roo to their first ever breakfast McMuffin. Sitting at the window looking outside at the blue sky it seemed incomprehensible that less than six hours ago we were facing an uncertain future and now we were all safe, happy and planning our next foray into another country, Italy.

Time to get back on the rollercoaster.

CHAPTER ELEVEN

I'M NOT THE ONLY IRRITATING CRITTER

Too expensive. Not safe. Miss it out. You'd be crazy to go there. These were the main recurring comments we kept reading about Italy. Thankfully we ignored these and spent an amazing five weeks travelling through this beautiful country. September was ideal in terms of the weather being cooler but still warm enough to walk around in shorts and t-shirt and it had the bonus of being quieter as many holidaymakers had headed back home.

The reason for ignoring the comments we had read on various sites was quite simple, Venice. We've always wanted to visit the floating city and when we were forced to leave Croatia because of the terrible storm, we found that Italy was our closest refuge.

This turned out to be our country number ten and reaching double figures was a milestone for us. It meant we felt we had cracked the travelling game and from here the only way was to keep going as it was easier than going back to the UK.

We have a life free of work stress, we were seeing some amazing sights and sharing experiences without it costing the earth. The life that we used to have was placed at the back of our minds and almost forgotten. Our current journey does however involve other stresses such as choosing which direction to head, finding a place for the night and the main stress of course, which is looking after Ozzie. Always up to mischief, in trouble or just being in the wrong place at the wrong time she really is a constant challenge.

We arrived in Venice on the 1st September and we chose to stay at the closest camper area to Venice, which was basically a concrete car park called Parcheggio del Tronchetto. It wasn't the cheapest place at 21 euro for first twelve hours and 16 euro for each subsequent twelve hours but it is certainly the most convenient and as we were only staying two nights it seemed perfect for our short visit and it turned out to be fine for what we wanted and needed.

Ozzie and Roo are well behaved dogs most of the time but visiting cities isn't their idea of fun and does stress them out so we made the decision for Venice and for other cities and tourist attractions to try and avoid busy times. This works both ways as we understand that most tourists don't want to share their space with dogs, no matter how cute and this is magnified in Venice as space is limited and at a premium.

Our first foray into Venice was late in the evening and the beauty and charm was evident from the moment we arrived. Despite being late evening the place was still busy with tourists, so we picked up a map from tourist information and took a seat at a small, and fairly cheap, local café. We discussed the places we wanted to visit and marked down on the map where these must-see sights were. The streets were still full of tourists as we finished our coffee, so we left and headed back to Teddy as it would have been far too challenging navigating the narrow streets, bridges and paths with both dogs.

This place was weird as there were hardly any areas to walk on and most of the space was filled with canals and boats. When we got there it was manic, full of tourists and this is one of the things I don't like about cities. The people and the crowds. Being at doggy height all you see is legs coming towards you and you get hit by people's bags and nudged and occasionally stepped on.

Roo being a little taller than me doesn't have as many issues with walking in a crowd but she too gets trod on which makes her give out an almighty yelp. Thankfully we didn't stay long in Venice and got back to Teddy that night where we rested and slept until the unusual and piercing sound of the alarm bell woke us. It was still dark outside and I turned to continue with my snooze until the familiar routine of watching Paul and Emma getting dressed meant we were off out.

Teddy was parked a twenty minute walk from the centre so we decided the best way to beat the crowds was to set our alarm for 5.30am the following morning. The difficulty in finding the alarm on the phone showed how long ago it had been since it was set and it was a painful reminder of days gone by. We woke to the sound of the alarm the next morning and felt surprisingly fresh and ready to go, with the exception of Ozzie who isn't really a morning person. Funnily enough she isn't really an evening person either. We were back in the centre of Venice by 6.15am and had the entire city to ourselves except for a few refuse collectors cleaning the streets. The city was absolutely deserted which allowed us to focus on the architecture and as the sun rose the beauty of this amazing city was intensified.

Apart from practically being the middle of the night, this visit to Venice was a better experience with no crowds and what a beautiful place this was. I got to be off my lead as there were no cars, just boats and Roo and I wandered through the narrow streets and across the small bridges, it was great having the place to ourselves. When in Venice you have to have an ice cream and Emma treated us to a cone each which Roo inhaled in seconds. Roo and I had to carry out our various poses for the all too familiar photo shots of our trip and for most of these I decided to turn my back as I was in that sort of mood.

After an amazing three hours touring the city we had seen enough for this visit and ticked off what we had come to see. We took plenty photos of the dogs at the Basilica di San Marco, St Mark's Square and the bridge of sighs. Just as the tourists reappeared, we found a café to refuel, where we were serenaded by a violinist playing oh sole mio. Some of you may know as a familiar tune from a popular ice cream advert. Having expected the worst in terms of prices, we were surprised to be charged less than six euro for two coffees and two admittedly tiny sandwiches. We sat and watched the tourists, busloads of them, arrive and head off towards the main sightseeing areas. Our work here was done and back to Teddy we wandered, pleased with ourselves as this city isn't big enough for tourists and the four of us. Well maybe it is but it isn't fair on anyone, least of all the dogs.

This was day 54 on the road and whilst we could have spent longer in Venice we had decided that it was a place that one day we would return to. Minus the dogs, minus Teddy and minus the 5.30am alarm call.

From Venice our map suggested a visit to Lake Garda would be a good idea and 90 minutes later we arrived in Peschiera at the southern end of the lake. The view and colour of the lake as we arrived was simply amazing and whilst it remained beautiful throughout our visit, the beauty of this initial glimpse was never quite repeated.

We arrived at the camper area planning on staying for a day or two and ended up staying for twelve as it was such as great place in every respect. The site had everything we needed, electricity, decent Wi-Fi, showers, spacious pitches, launderette, a Lidl close by and only a five minute walk into the town. All for 15 euro per night. For being such a popular resort, food and drink wasn't expensive either, a couple of euro for a glass of wine with free tapas and a meal out at a restaurant overlooking Lake Garda was around 35 euro for two.

From Peschiera you can take a boat trip to other resorts such as Garda and Bardolino and on day two we boarded and paid for a ferry trip, only to find that this was expensive at around 25 euro each. On holiday I imagine this is what you would expect to pay for a ferry trip on one of the famous Italian lakes but as we were on a never ending holiday this was a luxury and ate into our budget.

Tickets purchased we spent an enjoyable day mixing with the tourists around the lake and the dogs seemed to enjoy the short ferry trips though Roo was eager to jump overboard and into the crystal clear water. The next day we looked at options and decided upon a much cheaper mode of transport and caught the bus to a very beautiful and impressive town called Sirmione. The bus only took ten minutes, though as we boarded the driver indicated that both dogs needed muzzles on. We were unaware of the laws in place around this and we indicated we didn't have these. Thankfully the driver let us and the dogs on without them and after ten minutes passed we arrived without the driver putting any further pressure on us.

We spent a lovely afternoon walking around Sirmione with only a handful of tourists for company and Roo decided to entertain them by retrieving stones from the sea. For what seemed like hours, we sat on the sea wall and threw stone after stone into the sea and watched amazed as Roo raced after them. Submerging her head and neck into the water before returning to us with the same stone.

After a coffee and ice cream we took our place at the bus stop to make the short journey home. When I say short, I mean it was a short journey by bus. It would be a long walk if the driver this time insisted on seeing muzzles for the dogs. At this moment we both looked at each other and realised we had been enjoying the day and had forgotten about the muzzle situation. Thankfully we started speaking to another English couple at the bus stop and by the time arrived we boarded, we had again forgotten the dogs needed muzzles, and thankfully this time the driver didn't ask.

Marveling at the beauty of the lake on the bus ride home we agreed that this was another place we would like to visit, without the dogs. We also agreed that after visiting the neighbouring towns, they were all beautiful, although Peschiera was the best place on the lake for us.

We hopped on and off ferries and buses to visit places here which I didn't mind much although I did hear a bus driver say we had to wear a muzzle next time we get onto a bus. There was no way I was wearing a muzzle, I had seen them before on some other dogs and they look embarrassing. I have my street cred to think about and anyway how would I be able to eat poo and food scraps from the bins if I was wearing one of those things. Emma has bought these for us now and tried them on for size which was unbearable and I looked ridiculous. She soon took them off and at least we have these now just in case we make another bus trip.

This was the point in our trip when we also pushed on with our exercise routine. Only stopping in places for one or two nights had presented some problems in finding dog friendly walks and runs so it was good for us all to stay here for a while and get a chance to explore the area. Behind the town wall we found a never ending dog friendly canal path and spent every day running, walking and cycling there. Underneath a viaduct near the start of the path was a weekend pop up bar charging 1 euro for a very generous glass of whatever you fancied.

After eight weeks on the road this was also the first place we met people for long enough to have decent conversations, share advice and hopefully keep in touch with. At this stage we didn't have much advice to pass on so we enjoyed receiving advice from more seasoned travellers. Mal and Mary from Ireland who had a motorhome that seemed to have everything. Whilst we had previously survived on beer and red wine, any drink we wanted, Mal had and they even had ice!

Manfred and Susie from Koblenz in Germany continued the hospitality by inviting us to their motorhome for Spaghetti Bolognaise German style. This was cooked with white wine and was delicious and he also kept Paul supplied with super strength German beers which was an additional treat.

All in all Peschiera was a fantastic place and it was really good to feel and act like a tourist after weeks living in Teddy with only each other for company.

The running and walking we have done the last few days has been great, the track alongside the canal is a great run for all of us. It was similar to Holland in that there are cyclists so you had to dodge out the way but apart from that, this place was perfect.

The place where we stayed here was perfect too as it meant I could hop in and out of Teddy and go exploring nearby, providing I stayed within sight of Paul and Emma. There were also some other dogs around that I visited frequently and ate their food. Paul and Emma had also made some friends, one being an elderly man from Germany who came to visit us most evenings.

He had a large belly similar to mine and liked to eat and drink and drink. He would chat for hours about his interest in rollercoasters. Yes this man loved rollercoaster and to be honest this topic of conversation became quite boring after a while with him telling us all about the big dippers and theme parks he had visited in his lifetime.

Travelling allows you to meet people from all walks of life and in all shapes and sizes. I love meeting people and the madder and more eccentric they are the better. Whilst here we met a German pensioner with a passion for riding rollercoasters. He was on holiday here to visit the Gardaland theme park which was close by and we had also heard good reports about but thankfully the two dogs prevented us from visiting.

He was a lively character with so much energy and passion for theme parks. We asked him about his country and recommendations of where to go such as the Black Forest but he told us not to bother and instead go to the theme park. He knew everything about every rollercoaster in the world and I guessed that this would be his chosen subject if ever a contestant on Mastermind.

The various nationalities across Europe are all very different such as their mannerisms, and attitudes which I find differ quite considerably.

The Italians are notoriously flamboyant and like to be together and you see them in motorhomes lined up next to each other. They like to socialise and there's always lots of noise and laughter coming from their direction. Surprisingly the Italian motorhomes are generally quite old and not the largest ones you see on the road. They arrive and the motorhome door opens and a whole family pours out, the mother, father, numerous kids, the grandmother, grandfather, dogs, they just keep coming and I don't know how they all travel and sleep in such a small space.

We have Dutch friends who are very friendly and larger than life yet the motorhomers from the Netherlands we have come across tend to keep themselves to themselves. We haven't spoken to many people from there and they seem to prefer older motorhomes similar to the Italians.

The French seem to do a lot of travelling in motorhomes and what I like about their culture is the social lunches they have. They really make it a big thing at their meal times in particular lunch which is usually consists of a variety of foods and wines laid on a table and then they all congregate and eat together as a group. It is an extremely sociable event and one French couple we met in Portugal had fantastic looking lunches each day. She made all of the food herself in her tiny motorhome and even freshly made marmalade which she shared with us.

The German motorhomers we met have all been lovely, friendly warm people and always offer you a beer no matter what time of day it is. We find they like to follow the rules at all times and if a site asks you to pay before noon then they pay before 10am whereas other nationalities are more relaxed and would wait until noon or in some cases until they are asked to pay in the hope that they may get missed and bag a free night.

Whilst travelling Europe we've met people from all over the world some from as far away as Australia and also Finland, Norway, Hungary and even Russia. It's a great way to meet people and it's one of my hobbies now, a bit like train spotting but more motorhome spotting to see the registration plate to identify where they are from.

As soon as I see a GB sign on a number plate I like to go and introduce myself and find out where people are from and where they are going. I love meeting new people and for me this is the best part of travelling. It's always good to speak to people to get tips and advice on where to go and this has helped map out most of our trip. Finding out from other fellow travellers where to go, what to see and how best to get there. Since travelling I am more confident speaking to other nationalities as you learn and pick up some words and phrases and I always think it is nice to make an effort and greet people using their language.

We met an interesting couple whilst in Italy from the UK who had travelled for 16 months and were now house sitting for a friend. They had a cocker spaniel dog with them who was extremely well behaved but Ozzie soon led it astray as they wandered off into the woodland, close by to where we were standing chatting. Several attempts for them to retrieve their dog didn't work and she was puzzled and commented that her dog had never disobeyed her before. Obviously it was the influence of Ozzie that had caused her dog to misbehave.

She was worried for her dog whereas I'm used to having a Beagle that vanishes into thin air and so I was more laid back. I offered to go and find them and started heading towards the woodland with a lead in my hand. I had only taken fifty steps when I saw it.

A snake! It was curled up and was of medium size and was a dark green colour with yellow flecks. I screamed, turned and ran away from it. The woman still concerned for her cocker spaniel warned me that snakes had been spotted in the area due to the climate and because they breed at this time of year and populated this area. She told me a tale of the viperidae (a viper) snake that had been spotted and seemingly if you are bitten you have two hours to get medical help or it is too late.

I thought to myself, the dogs can remain lost as I wasn't prepared to walk any further to find them but could see them both close by and treats from my pocket tempted them both back.

Later that day a google search confirmed that what she said was true and it also showed up images of this viperidae snake. Sending a shiver down my spine I was shocked to see it looked like the exact one I had seen and very nearly stepped on. Guess I had been lucky not to have trodden on this, especially in my flip flops!

Snakes are not on my list of favourite creatures, especially ones that can kill you. During our time backpacking around Australia we came across a few, one being a poisonous brown snake that I spotted on the bathroom ceiling whilst Paul was having a shower. Even at this time, when I expected him to panic, he continued with his shower, casually getting out before assessing the situation.

Whilst in Italy we were always out and about in fields, hills and mountains with the dogs so were a little worried about the snakes that we had heard about. The tips on the internet said that at this time of year stay away from mountains, fields, grass and waste land, basically everywhere. It advised you to always wear trousers and I guess snakes are deterred by people wearing trousers. Then my mind wandered to a brilliant invention to prevent people from being bitten by snakes. I could design specially designed pants that have a repellent in them and patent them "snake pants" very popular for the male population I think.

So my flip flops had to go and out came the walking boots and trousers as I wasn't leaving anything to chance and so took all of the precautions. Snake awareness taken on board and fully equipped to deal with these, we were then led to another irritating critter. No, not Ozzie, this time in the form of tics.

I could feel one of those critters bite me and was going mad with the irritation and pain. They nipped me all over my body and they hurt. The thing with tics is that they cling to your skin and stay there sucking the blood from you. No matter how hard I tried they just don't come off so Emma has to take them off for me using her tweezers.

One of the tics had found a home in my bottom and it was uncomfortable when I sat so I had to adjust my usual sitting pose and lean more to one side. Clearly this tic had grown to like me and had also grown quite considerably in size which increase by the minute due to the amount of blood it was sucking from me. In fact it grew so large that I couldn't sit for long periods and had to stand. I hate these creatures and they are not welcome on my body anymore especially not on my bottom.

There were tics everywhere, horrible little things and we kept finding them on Ozzie and luckily I had tweezers with us to remove them. This has to be done in a particular way to pinch and twist them as you remove them so you get the full body including the head as they bury this into the skin first to suck the blood.

At first I didn't realise what they were until I took a closer look at one of them on Ozzie that had latched itself to her neck and looking closely you could see small legs sprouting from it. After my initial investigation I was shocked to keep finding more and more of them. From the first one successfully removed from her neck this continued with me having to remove well over twenty of them in one sitting. This was an operation de-ticking session where Ozzie sat very still and allowed me to pluck them from her. I think she was relieved to have these taken from her as she doesn't usually allow me this much air time.

It is one of the most revolting tasks to do and I was retching and gagging as one by one I plucked them from her skin. From this point Paul and I took turns to remove these as this was just gut wrenching at times and also took up time as it took an age to get them all off her.

Once we were confident all tics had been removed we took the dogs for a walk and noticed Ozzie was walking differently with a kind of strut. Taking wider steps and spreading her back legs apart, walking like a diva, imagine Beyoncé doing a twerk and you get the idea. Paul and I couldn't stop laughing as she looked ridiculous. I stopped her to see why on earth she was walking differently, and what was causing her to shake her bootie.

On inspection I checked her paws, claws and hind legs and found nothing there until I noticed a huge tic that had literally attached itself to her backside. It was massive and was obviously in its element having been there for goodness knows how long as I could see it had already collected a large sac of blood from her. It was about the size and colour of a blackberry fruit pastel and as a result from this has totally put me off eating these again, ever.

We didn't have our tweezers with us so continued our walk where Paul and I had a lengthy discussion of whose turn it was to remove the tic this time. Knowing I was going to get this job I wasn't looking forward to it. So Ozzie continued to strut her stuff until we got back to the motorhome where the removal began.

Tweezers in hand, the look of fear in Ozzie's face told me she wasn't looking forward to this too. She whimpered and ran away not wanting me near her so not to stress her anymore. I left her until she eventually settled and she managed to do this by sitting side saddle on her favourite seat.

I waited until she was asleep and tried again to retrieve it and with success and in the midst of her sleep the tic was removed and discarded. Ozzie woke as soon as I plucked it from her with her face meeting mine. Never really showing much affection towards me, a lick from her on my cheek I think was her way of saying thank you.

I am such a hardy animal with a solid frame and an endless supply of stamina. Before we left home Emma took Roo and I to the vets to get checked over and to get our passports for this trip. The vet examined me as I stood on his table and I allowed him to feel my bones, ribs and stomach, he gave my hind legs a squeeze and checked out my teeth and gums also. He put a stopper thing on my chest and said this was to check my heart.

During this the vet looked at me straight in the eye and said "wow"... Oh no I thought what does that mean was it not ticking or was I going to die? Was this time for me to be dust? This is how it all started with Miffy. My anxiety kicked in and the knots in my stomach returned with a vengeance.

Turning to Emma he asked if I exercised. Of course, I run and run every day with Paul, in fact I run everywhere. Why was he asking these ridiculous questions? He still had the stopper thing on my chest and looked at me again and said "Ozzie you are one fit dog your heart rate has the beat of a top athlete". Phew this was good news, so I'm not going to die then?

Moments of panic flashed past me and then turned to joy. He gave Roo and I medicine in the form of an injection to prevent us from getting any nasty illnesses and a collar to stop anymore tics but these need to be changed every few months so my tic infestation could have been prevented as my collar had obviously expired.

I know I have caused upset to Paul and Emma with these awful nipping tics. I don't mean for them to bite and live on me like they do and I do not want to be a burden as I heard them debate who had to remove them. Luckily I haven't had as many of these nip me since Paul bought me a new collar and hopefully these will stay away from me now.

CHAPTER TWELVE

ALL AT SEA

Being in Italy had given us time to reflect on our trip to date. We both realised that we had encountered numerous highs and lows along the way and this came to the fore on route to Santini Vineyard in Coriano.

Whilst driving on the motorway towards our spot for the night Teddy suddenly stopped mid-way through a tunnel and Paul desperately tried to fire the engine up again and again but Teddy had given up, there was no life in him.

Being stuck in a tunnel, on a motorway was not a good place to break down! The sound of horns was deafening around us. We braced ourselves for the inevitable thud from a lorry or car as we knew that being stationery in this spot was extremely hazardous.

Paul tried desperately to turn the key in the hope the engine would fire up and eventually the little life that was left in the engine got us moving out of the tunnel and he just managed to limp into an escape lane at the side of the motorway. The traffic sped past us at breaking speed as I tentatively slid out the door and walked the short distance to the breakdown phone nearby, leaving Paul and the dogs in Teddy.

The controller on the other end of the phone didn't speak English and I didn't speak Italian, so this resulted in me having to decipher what on earth she was saying. I was stumped as to how on earth I could sort this out, as there was no Wi-Fi around us and I couldn't think of a way of finding a translator to help. Heading back to Teddy, disheartened and wondering what on earth we could do my spirits rose when I saw a tow truck had pulled behind us where we were parked.

The mechanic jumped out of his van and approached us started speaking incredibly fast to us. As if on purpose trying to confuse us by not using separate words, just one long continuous word that went on and on. There was no way of communicating with him or understanding anything he said. My friend Nellie from the UK, speaks Italian fluently after living there for many years so I called her and thankfully she answered. I explained what had happened and she agreed to help so I passed the phone to the mechanic. Several, ci,ci, no, no's later he passed the phone back to me. Nellie confirmed that he was going to tow us off the motorway and it would cost 200 euro.

We really didn't have any other option, so agreed and in no time we were hooked up onto the back of his tow truck and towed from the layby to safety of a garage, which was literally 150 yards away. Yes, this minimal distance of 150 yards cost us 200 euro! The mechanic at the garage took one look at Teddy and informed us that we had ran out of diesel. I know you will now be shaking your head at how ridiculous this is, I felt the same.

Annoyed and frustrated that we had wasted 200 euro just because we had ran out of fuel, we filled the tank and desperately wanted to get to our spot for the night as it was getting dark and late. Literally twenty minutes later we found ourselves parked at Santini vineyard where there are several parking spots for motorhomes.

We had the most bizarre couple of days. Firstly Paul decided to stop Teddy in a tunnel on a motorway whilst other vehicles sped past us. Why he did this I don't know. I do know that it was a stupid decision as there was no walking routes for Roo and I. Paul must have went on strike and refused to move as Emma made a phone call and a very fast speaking Italian man came in a large truck and we rode on the back of him as his truck pulled us along. Thankfully we quickly reached a place where we could walk which was on a vineyard.

With the place to ourselves and amazing views in the distance of San Marino our first impression was that it was pretty magnificent. We urgently required electricity and Wi-Fi and couldn't get either to work and then the owner arrived and he sorted this out for us.

His name was Sandro and he immediately made us feel very welcome and explained that we were to use all of the facilities in his home, including the washing machine, toilet, shower and his swimming pool.

After a good night's sleep and lengthy discussion over the small incident of breaking down the previous day we put the leads on the dogs and attempted to take them for a walk. I say attempted as twenty metres into the walk Sandro appeared and our education about wine production began.

Sandro was passionate about his vineyard and rightly so as this was an amazing place to live as well as being his livelihood. He took us on a tour of the vineyard, and his house, which has two guest rooms that he rents out to guests. We ended this tour in the kitchen with a tasting session of the six bottles of wine that Sandro produces, plus his own olive oil and enough meat and cheese to soak up the alcohol. A few hours later and slightly inebriated we walked the twenty metres back to Teddy with two confused looking dogs wondering what on earth had happened to their walk.

The following day we had our leads clipped on and Roo and I were excited to get out and explore, only for this supposed walk to stop within a matter of steps of leaving Teddy. We spent most of the day in the kitchen at the vineyard and I could see Paul and Emma getting tipsier from each mouthful they took. I know this because they were given copious amounts of red stuff and then white stuff to drink. When Emma drinks the red stuff her voice goes much louder and she can become really annoying. They had cheese, ham and salami and more cheese, ham and salami and it was delicious. The more they drank the more food I got as this just kept falling from the table and on reflection it was much better than a walk anyway.

We found out that harvesting was due to take place in three days' time, weather permitting, and it was maybe the alcohol or maybe genuine interest that saw us volunteer with the grape picking. The following Monday we found ourselves standing next to the vines alongside ten or so professional pickers. This was a great experience to meet the locals and to also be contributing to supporting Sandro with his wine producing business. The grapes we picked will be used to make his next batch of wine and our name will be forever associated with the 2015 wine from Santini.

The town of Coriano was a fifteen minute walk along quiet roads and whilst pretty enough we didn't venture there too often as we had everything we needed at the vineyard. Motorbike fanatics may be interested in the memorial to rider Marco Simoncelli who died at the Malaysian Grand Prix in 2011 that is erected in the village square. Sitting at the poolside at the vineyard allowed us to hear the roar of bikes in the distance from the 2014 San Marino Grand Prix, won fittingly by an Italian, Valentino Rossi.

From here we took day trips to San Marino where we ate the most amazing pizza whilst overlooking the grand vistas of the country side her that stretched for as far as the eye can see. We also visited Rimini and were surprised with the great beaches there and also designate areas solely for dogs that had numerous agility equipment there for them to play on.

Travelling in a motorhome really makes you appreciate the simple things in life, for instance water. Buying bottled water can prove to be costly and we found ourselves constantly confused by the amount of variety on offer with fizz, a little fizz or without fizz (still). So we were overjoyed when we found a water filling machine that charged only 5 centimos per litre in the centre of Coriano. It was cold, still and tasted perfect. These were the types of things that made us happy when on the road and I'm sure those motorhomers amongst you reading this would agree also.

How we were the only motorhome here at Tenuta Santini during the eight night stay will remain a mystery to us, as without doubt this was one of the best camper places we had visited on our trip. Leaving this place was hard to do and we could have and really should have stayed longer but we wanted to get to other parts of Italy and to be on the road to explore again.

Upon leaving we purchased all six bottles of wine and a bottle of olive oil which we enjoyed at further special places on our trip. Total bill for accommodation and wine was around the same as one night in a decent hotel in the UK. Long live the motorhome. The memories and happy times we spent there make it a place we will definitely be returning to hopefully in the very near future.

From Coriano we visited a small seaside town called Lesina on the east coast of Italy. At first it looked beautiful and a perfect place to stop for the night. The camping spot was free with no facilities but was literally right on the beach, it was the end of the season, very quiet with only us parked up for the evening.

Paul was tired from driving as Connie had taken us off route again whilst we were trying to find a Lidl store for food supplies. We usually get ourselves lost at least once on each journey due to numerous factors, and end up heading in the wrong direction to where we want to be. We also had countless episodes and challenges, to include height restrictions, one way roads or bridges with weight or width restrictions.

Often Connie would inform us that we had reached our destination whilst driving on the motorway or she would ask us to do a U-turn just as we arrived at the camping spot. She incessantly annoyed us but we still continued to use her polite speaking navigation service as my map reading skills are somewhat hopeless. We found ourselves taking to her in the hope we would annoy her off as much as she was annoying us, by saying "no Connie, you are wrong", and "no Connie I'm not doing a U-turn no matter how many times you ask us to".

We had found a suitable spot and Paul was chilling out and happily we felt settled for the night. The sun was still shining, the waves crashing close to us and I was dying to get out for a run. Ozzie and Roo were too rearing to go and yelped with excitement as they watched me change into my running kit. This always gives them the indication that I am taking them out and this trigger makes them go wild with excitement.

The beach, as far as I could see, looked really beautiful and appealing but literally five minutes into my run and further along the coastline it became dirty, really dirty with piles and piles of rubbish littered everywhere.

We later found that there had been some storms in this area the previous week so I would expect some rubbish to have been washed up but this place was like a dumping site. Old tyres, pieces of wood, sinks, bottles sanitary waste and I even spotted numerous syringes, it really was disgusting. Further into my run the rubbish grew more and more which made it impossible to walk never mind run so eventually I had no choice but to turn back.

This place was dirty, there was glass everywhere and Roo and I had to be careful not to cut our paws. I didn't like this beach it smelt funny and I knew Emma didn't like it too as we soon turned and ran back to Teddy. It was our dinner time anyway and I put an extra spurt on to get there first. Just as we arrive back, my favourite person had our dinner ready and served it to us immediately, he is just the greatest.

After a very peaceful night with not a soul around us we were woken by the sound of crashing waves on the shore. It was yet another beautiful day so we were up and out in no time to explore more of this town to wander in the hope of finding a café, bar or restaurant for some breakfast.

Within minutes of walking we arrived at the small town and immediately felt uneasy about the place. All of the shops and restaurants were closed or boarded up. It was filthy dirty just the same as the beach, the buildings were all grey and run down and it looked like a war zone. There were no people here at all, no one to be seen in any of the streets, houses or gardens. Just hordes of stray dogs roaming the streets and all looking very sorry for themselves. It was such a sad and depressing sight to see and not one we would have ever linked to Italy. Grey shabby concrete block houses, no grass, no trees, no greenery, no flowers, basically this place was colourless and a complete contrast to the other places we had visited in this country.

As always we kept our spirits high in the hope of finding some sort of life and kept wandering through the streets looking out for a place that was open. We approached a bend in the road and thought this is where it would all be happening. We fantasised about seeing restaurants, cafes and wine bars but to our disappointment it was just the same, dull grey and boring lifeless shabby streets.

Noticing two very large canisters hissing gas out at an almighty speed filled the air with a revolting toxic smell and this was our sign to turn and go back to Teddy which we did wanting to take the quickest route possible which took us alongside the beach front.

I really didn't like it here and especially the smell that made me feel quite ill. Roo and I saw other dogs in the streets and they were all sitting down and huddled together. I could see that the dogs looked thin and you could see their bones, they look sad and some of them were very ugly, making me look quite beautiful in comparison.

My anxiety returned here and that awful knot I get in my stomach told me this was not a happy place. As I walked past the poor ugly dogs, they had so much sadness in their eyes and I wondered why they didn't look happy. I approached one to see if I could cheer him up but he didn't want me in his face and as a warning showed me his teeth. Well what he had of teeth anyway as all I saw was his gums and only a few cracked and broken teeth.

We wouldn't recommend you making a visit to this place unless you have a fascination for pollution, toxic waste or dilapidated architecture. It was difficult to imagine what this place looked like in the summer months when we were told it would be packed out with tourists. There were hotels and holiday homes here but unfortunately they just looked very tired and old and in much need of a refurbishment.

On our route back to Teddy we agreed it best to leave this place. The sea was angry and rough and as we walked along the beachfront the view of the ocean was spoilt by the amount of waste and rubbish that had been washed onto the beach. We must have walked for further than we thought as an hour later we still weren't at Teddy and starting to grow impatient we arrived at a large inlet that ran from the village sewers into the sea.

I'm not a very confident swimmer and wasn't keen on wading through the water, it was dirty, a murky colour plus I do not like the sea at all as I'm frightened of what might be in there to bite me. As my most loved comedian Billy Connolly would say "stay out of the sea, we don't belong in there" and I have always followed his advice.

All four of us stood looking at ways in which we could cross this inlet and threw a stone in to gauge how deep it was which confirmed that yes it was fairly deep. Roo who loves the water showed apprehension too which made us think we should turn back and take the extended detour back through the derelict town, but the thought of returning to the sad old town was too depressing to consider.

There was a man close to the inlet fishing who had been watching us and he shouted to get our attention. His hands demonstrating for us to go and see him. He was offering to help us cross the inlet and I waved my arms to indicate the no gesture and mimed that I was not a good swimmer and acted out that I was drowning. He laughed at us but was persistent as he jumped into the sea to show us the depth of the water. Still wearing his jeans and shirt he was soaked to the skin. His demonstration didn't help and only made things worse as the inlet was way too deep, up to his waist in fact, so I suggested that it would be better for us all to turn back.

After much discussion the fisherman really wouldn't take no for an answer. He wasn't going to give up so we decided the only way for me to get over was to climb on Paul's back so I wouldn't get wet.

I checked my phone was safe in the pocket of my shirt, jumped on Paul's back and felt safer up high for a moment, but as soon as we entered the water my feet and legs were submerged and I could feel a strong pull of the water dragging us towards the ocean. It was only a few metres to cross this inlet but for Paul it was physically challenging especially with me on his back. I was shrieking hysterically with fear as we neared the safety of the other side and almost there when the current caught us and made us both fall into the water, my iPhone included! By this time the fisherman was laughing uncontrollably at us and was literally doubled over and howling with amusement as we stood there soaked to the skin.

So there I was just left on the other side of the inlet whilst Paul and Emma got themselves over safely. I willed for them to come and get me as I've never really tried swimming and I know that I do not like the sea. It was pointless them constantly shouting my name to cross as I didn't want to get into the water. I thought Roo would have helped me but she was off and jumped athletically into the water swimming across like a true professional. She is a great swimmer and so confident, unlike me! She should have webbed feet the amount of swimming she does.

I dipped one of my paws into the cold water and I felt it sink into the sand, trying to wriggle it free the weight of my body made it sink further and further leaving me no option but to go for it. I stretched and paddled my paws like mad that propelled me forward amazed with myself that I was afloat and was actually swimming.

It was however an awful experience and my heart was beating faster and faster with each paddle I made, the water kept going into my mouth and it tasted terrible. My constant paddling was exhausting and I really wasn't getting anywhere, resulting in me being dragged in completely the wrong direction. Not towards the calls from Paul and Emma but in the direction of the ocean and the horizon, the waves were strong and the current pulled my body into the depths of the sea.

You can imagine by this time my anxiety was in full throttle I couldn't breathe, my head was constantly being dunked under the water. I was growing weaker by the second and my pathetic attempts at doggy paddle had slowed. No matter how hard I tried I couldn't move any further and was burnt out with no energy left at all, I was exhausted.

My fleeting last memory of this event was the distant sight of Paul, Emma and Roo stood on the beach that I could only barely make out, just looking like small dots on the landscape. I had been taken out quite a distance away from them and although I could hear their calls my vision became blurred and confusion set in.

I thought my days were over and this was my time to be turned to dust. I felt warm knowing that this was my end and wasn't afraid knowing that now I would eventually be reunited with Miffy. My head now fully submerged in the depths of the water and I could feel the sensation in my body being drifted further and further out to sea. It was at this point I felt my collar being pulled and lifting my head I saw there was a hand attached to me that was dragging me with it and taking me to shore.

Reaching the beach and being reunited with my family was overwhelming. They did look relieved to have me back and Roo too showed her love for me as she nudged past me only to eat the huge pile of sick that I had brought up.

As usual poor Ozzie got her timings all wrong on her approach to cross the inlet. Just as she entered the water a wave came and took her out to sea. She was swept out into the depths of the murky waters and all we could see was her tiny head bobbing up and down. Luckily the very kind fisherman who had at this point stopped his hysterical laughing, swam out to her and caught hold of her collar then dragging her with him as he swam back to shore with her. He really was our hero of the day and in fact saved Ozzie's life.

She was clearly shaken by this and she looked exhausted, with her ears hanging lower than usual due to the excess water they had absorbed, her eyes all a glaze. I think she got a real fright and we did too. Thanking and hugging the fisherman for his life saving skills we were all soaked to the skin and continued our walk back to Teddy with the words from Paul "let's get out of this place". By the look of Ozzie, if she could talk she would have said the same thing!

Once we reached Teddy we got dried off and changed, packed up and headed south west across Italy towards Sorrento.

The Amalfi coast was another place that we have always wanted to visit so we were thrilled to reach this beautiful harbour town with stunning scenery that exceeded our expectations. Manoeuvring the motorhome through the winding streets and steep inclines was quite challenging and in the distance we thankfully saw a campsite where we pulled in for the evening.

We couldn't find any motorhome stops so a campsite was our only option and whilst it was a little more extravagant that what we are used to the views of the coastline made it worthwhile. After getting our money's worth from using as many of the facilities as possible we ventured out to find a nice restaurant and to experience some authentic Italian delights. The footpath from the campsite into Sorrento was non existent so we took a chance and walked the 15 minutes or so at the side of a winding road.

It was a weekend and the small town was electric with people wandering in every direction, looking in shops and filling the bars and cafes. There were plenty of traders selling local crafts, the usual stuff, like leather belts, matching salt and pepper sets and lace place mats. Ideal presents for those loved ones at home.

We stumbled across a lovely restaurant with outdoor seating and the friendly waiter made us welcome and brought some water for the dogs. After ordering drinks we browsed the menu and found the prices somewhat extortionate. We looked at each other in silence and then discussed our options. These boiled down to paying for the drinks and leaving, sharing a starter and then leaving, or what the heck we're in Italy. The latter won and the pizzas soon arrived and we were surprised that they looked nor tasted anything like we would get back home. For example they weren't stacked with copious amounts of meat, vegetables and cheese but instead made with love, with good quality Italian ingredients and were delicious. We could easily have eaten two each but our budget was already being stretched.

We had a lovely evening there and arrived back at Teddy happy and content but still a little hungry. That night brought with it a heavy presence of humidity so much so it was like sleeping in a sauna. We were sticky and sweaty and Ozzie and Roo were struggling too.

I was sweating and no matter how much I panted to release this I just became hotter and hotter. Roo lay on the floor beneath me and I watched her as her chest heaved to catch some air. The windows and vents were open and usually cold air comes in but instead this was hot air not cooling me down one little bit. I could hear Emma complaining to Paul about the heat and none of us got much sleep that night.

The sun rose and yes the humidity was still there, we needed to get out of here and quick. My body had no energy through lack of sleep and because of the heat and I lay in a trance fixated on a small cluster of ants that were on the floor in Teddy and they were making their way towards the cupboards.

What is usually a calm and peaceful time at breakfast was shattered by screams from Emma as I watched her go to cupboard to get the cereal and our dog food and was greeted by thousands of ants that were happily munching on and stealing our food.

During our one night in Sorrento we were the target of thousands of ants that had decided to make Teddy their home. They were everywhere including our hair, our bed, in all the cupboards and in all of our cutlery and pans. Breakfast scrapped, Paul and I started the long laborious task of the fumigation procedure, basically throwing everything out, cleaning and replacing. We managed to eliminate most of the ants but some diehards stayed with us for a few weeks after this and I wonder how they felt about their new home in France.

Our next stop was further north and the campsite was ideally situated directly opposite the ruins of Pompeii. Again it was a red hot day and within minutes of arriving and parking Teddy, Ozzie and Paul were stretched out in the blistering heat. I rolled the awning out for some shade but they both moved back into the sun.

Watching them both dozing in the mid-day sun reminded me of the expression "mad dogs and Englishmen" and Ozzie is certainly one mad dog.

We waited until 4pm to visit when it was a little cooler as it was too hot to do anything through the day.

It was the right decision to visit later in the day as it was quiet and most of the street sellers and tourists had packed up and gone which meant we practically had the place to ourselves.

Pompeii is an amazing place to visit and if you have never been then get your bags packed now and go. Most of these ancient remains from the volcanic eruption in 79AD are in perfect condition allowing you to see exactly what it used to look like and the restoration work that is ongoing is brilliant even allowing you to enter some of the buildings that still showed the murals on the walls. An added bonus for us was that it's a dog friendly place and lots of strays live there and seem to have made it their home.

We did a full tour of the site and stood up high on one of the monuments and watched as the sun set which reflected on the ruins around us. The glow from this gave the place a new perspective where shadows were formed and an eerie atmosphere was created. We found it to be such a magical place the stillness and peacefulness and the amazing backdrop of Mount Vesuvius made it all the more special.

This place was great. We had so many nooks and crannies to explore and it smelt different to other places we had been to. Roo is always so friendly with other dogs and headed straight to visit a pack of them showing no fear and giving them all a good sniff and made friends with them all instantly.

I however kept my distance from these as one of them looked at me in a way that brought on my anxiety. I was fine just sniffing and keeping one eye on Roo too. As I was sniffing I noticed a very long thing and it was following me.

It was a snake and a very large one at that and annoyingly it made its way in-between my legs, and I accidentally trod on it which it didn't like. I tried to out run it but it kept up and followed me.

We stood in the ruins of a theatre which gave Roo some time to make friends with the many dogs that lived there, all in different shapes and sizes and all quite friendly. There was actually a small charity called Pet Connection that allows you to adopt a dog or to make a donation which pleased me knowing that there was some sort of support for them.

I could see Ozzie giving the stray dogs a wide birth and was shocked to see she was distracted by what looked like a snake. I shouted for her to return and she immediately about turned and headed back to us. As she approached us we noticed she did indeed have company and yes we were right, it was a snake. You may remember that I do not like snakes and I reacted in what I thought to be a rational way screaming and running away as fast as my flip flops could take me and I didn't stop until I knew it had gone. Ozzie was clearly puzzled with me shouting for her to return only for me to then sprint off in the distance.

From Pompeii we drove the following day to Mount Vesuvius which was up a steep winding incline that took under an hour to reach the parking spot at the top where hundreds of tourists and coaches were already there. It was early morning and we wanted to get here before the crowds but on this occasion they beat us. The climb to the top was exhausting and we made our way weaving in-between the many people and reaching the crater in time for the clouds to lift to see the magnificent views. This was a quick visit though provided another tick on our list of places we wanted to visit.

From Pompeii our route north took us via Naples which turned out to be a culture shock for us all. It was Sunday morning and the streets were full with people begging, and living in small run down shacks. Teddy moved along slowly in the traffic heading towards our campsite for the night. We noticed that the streets looked so different to others we had seen in Italy and this area reminded us a lot of our trip to Kenya where we went for our honeymoon. There was so much poverty evident and you could see this from the buildings around us which were all boarded up with broken windows, the place was covered in litter which made it a real depressing sight.

The traffic lights on this stretch of road changed regularly and approaching these they seemed to turn to red more often than green. We waited patiently in the traffic when a well-built man appeared at our window desperate to get our attention and he was then joined by several other people, all surrounding us giving Teddy the once over.

The man still standing at the window followed us as we moved slowly but steadily inch by inch wishing the traffic lights would change to green for long enough to get away. He was demanding that we buy his produce which looked like grilled aubergines, but the last thing I wanted at that point was a roasted vegetable. Some olives, possibly, a large glass of wine, definitely, but on this occasion and in this heat, I couldn't be tempted by his limp looking legumes.

By this time we had a large gathering of vendors circling us trying to sell random items ranging from lighters, caps, umbrellas and matches, all of which we didn't need. Eventually after the longest ever traffic light stop we literally saw red and went for it straight through and onwards away from the sellers pestering us.

Literally twenty yards along the road we arrived at yet more traffic lights seemingly stuck on red, which brought with it more street sellers and would you believe it, the man selling aubergines was there again too. We must have been his main target and I gave in and wound the window down to give him a couple of euro's in exchange for a slippery inedible piece of veg that even the dogs wouldn't eat. Thinking that this would stop his persistence was proved wrong as it only made him keener to try and sell me more. It was a relief to get away as his constant staring and high pressure sales techniques stressed us out.

After loving every part of Italy to date this was such a culture shock for us and I can only think we took a wrong which had unfortunately led us to this area. Connie had taken us the scenic route again and for some reason we still continue to put all of our trust in the damn thing. Once our trip is over it is going on eBay!

Roo and I were sitting in the back and I strained my neck to get to see where we were but this place didn't look familiar at all. We parked up and Roo and I hopped out for our pee pee's and I instantly felt the heat from the sun on my back which felt good. It was nice, being free and out of Teddy. I lay on my back to get some sun on my tummy whilst Roo continued to interrupt me, wanting to play but I gave her a look that told her to stay away. That is all it takes for her to leave me alone and it works every time.

Enjoyable nights followed in Siena and Florence and this was memorable as being the only place where I have been able to smell wine in the air. The sheer amount of vineyards around the Chianti area fills the surrounds with the sweetest, most beautiful smells you can imagine.

Next stop was Pisa which we had never managed to visit previously due to the limited flights from Newcastle. Having Teddy gave us the chance to visit the leaning tower.

We were woken up early this morning and all I knew was that we were going to see a very tall building that leaned slightly. I wasn't sure it was going to be worth getting up at 6am for, however Paul, Emma and Roo wanted to go so I was outvoted. We had stayed on a camping spot close to the city centre but we still had to walk the forty five minutes to see the building. On arrival I was surprised to see it was busy with lots of tourists who as always liked to step on my paws.

Thankfully we didn't stay long and after lots of very similar photographs were taken, we headed back to Teddy and to our next destination. It didn't take long until we found somewhere to stop and on arrival Emma jumped out, performed the walk and found us a spot. Teddy was settled and levelled out for the night and I was happy to see Paul collect our leads and we were soon out in the cool air and exploring this place.

It was amazing here, the smells in the grass drove me wild. These were new smells that I had never experienced before. My taste buds were going mad and I ran and caught up with Roo who had raced ahead of me as I sniffed around to soak up all of the scents. We reached a steep incline which went on forever and I raced up all of the way to the top without stopping and dodging all of the obstacles that were in my way. My energy was cranked up to full and I had a spring in my step. I had noticed that my anxieties had faded and I hadn't been as bad lately with the knots in my stomach and constant worrying and realised this gave me a feeling of contentment and happiness. It felt quite good.

Up ahead I could see a clearing and headed for this. Roo was by my side now and just managing to keep up. Once we had both reached the top we were greeted by a pack of other hounds that lived there. They looked like me apart from bring scruffier, most of them were slightly taller than me and none of them wore a collar. They gave us a good sniff concentrating mostly on our bottoms and this soon confirmed that we were welcomed into the pack.

Hanging out with these other hounds was great fun and I was in my element as apparently I had been appointed top dog and as I raced ahead I noticed I was in the lead and the others followed behind me. This was great, and had never happened to me before. We stopped for a while to rest and we lay stretched out in the sunshine.

As I lay soaking up the rays one by one the hounds came and licked and kissed my face and belly. This was just delicious and I was in my element, anxieties, what anxieties? I stupidly, thought that these were my new friends, though my status of top dog was short lived and was shattered by the loud howling noise coming from the distance.

This howl got louder and opening my eyes I turned to see a huge black shadow of a dog towering over me. By this time my licking and kissing from the other dogs had stopped and they had all disappeared taking Roo with them.

I didn't know who this dog was and didn't wait around long enough to find out. Our eyes met and he didn't look pleased that I was in his spot and had been playing top dog with his friends. Of course I tried to play it cool but sensed that I shouldn't hang around. I casually rolled onto my side, picked myself up and raced off as fast as my little legs could take me in the direction of Paul and Emma who were sitting with Roo fairly close by. My fleeting moment of being a top dog in the pack was short lived. It felt great at the time but I quickly realised that there was always going to be someone bigger and more dominant just around the corner and I don't want to be in that position again. Having one dog to keep in line is hard enough.

Pisa was uneventful in that not much happened. The leaning tower had long been on my list of places to visit and as usual we headed in to the centre early morning. It ticked a box and I was pleased we had stopped off for a couple of days and had the chance to see it. The rest of Pisa we didn't really give much of a chance as we were keen to head north. Our walking in Italy had been trimmed back with us being a little more apprehensive due to the snake sightings we had encountered.

Leaving Pisa we drove to Deiva Marina and managed to pull into a campsite, check in, set Teddy up and head out for a walk in record time. As we watched the dogs race past us I reassured myself that if there were any snakes here, surely the dogs would be shooing them away for us. The walks in this area were strenuous and exhausting as the heat had increased and had become extremely hot.

We were heading up a mountain and stopped a few times to take in the views which were amazing and they highlighted the coast and clear blue waters that stretched for miles and miles. Once we reached the top of the mountain the dogs were greeted by a few waifs and strays that ran eagerly towards us. They followed us up the path and guarded their territory with precaution. They were friendly enough and Ozzie and Roo loved the attention and there was lots of bottom sniffing going on. This is where Ozzie found her calling as top dog and we watched with smiles on our faces as the power of this went to her head. She had all of the waifs and strays from the village following her as she strutted her stuff. Her tail was high in the air but unfortunately no sooner had she been crowned top dog when the mighty ruler in the form of a very large cross bred Alsatian moved her on, putting her back in her correct ranking.

Continuing with our walk we spotted a sign on the tree which said hog hunting to start first of October (the following day), all paths will be closed until December for hunting! We were lucky we had managed this walk and saw the views as the following day all paths would close for the hunting. We had to shield this sign from Ozzie in fear she might start to feel anxious about it after the events from Croatia where she was very nearly taken from us.

Deiva Marina was a small harbour town called situated on the west coast of Italy and the campsite was less than a two minute walk to the beach. This is where we bumped into some familiar people as again our paths kept crossing. A couple from Germany we had met in Florence turned up and parked next to us. Fred Frank and his wife, whose name I couldn't pronounce. I called him Fred Frank as I could never remember if he was called Fred or Frank hence he adopted a double barreled name which he quite liked. A fascinating couple who in their seventies had an air of sophistication, getting dressed very smartly for dinner each evening though they did spoil this by wearing their dressing gowns to the beach. The stories they told us of their travels through Africa in their twenties were inspirational.

There were some beautiful buildings in the town centre and a promenade that was being refurbished whilst we were there. The dogs were exhausted after their day walking up and over mountains as we had spent most of the day exploring. They were fed and quickly fast asleep, not even waking when the pizza box opened, as we had decided to get a take away that night. No cooking and no clearing up is always welcome when living in a motorhome.

The next morning we woke early and couldn't wait to get out as the sun was shining and it was another glorious day. As usual Paul and I got our running kit on which always excites Roo as she knows this means she will be going out. Roo always yelps and jumps at me and I try desperately to find my trainers, collect poo bags and leads before I am whisked out of the motorhome half-dressed and still putting my trainers on.

We set off along the promenade and onto the seafront. The dogs were just ahead of us and Roo was desperate to head into the sea and waited patiently for my command for her to go in. This was a great run and a good start to the day. Afterwards we stopped off near a moored boat to do some stretching and to take in the view. Both dogs were racing towards us and I could see water dripping from Roo from her morning dip in the sea, riding the waves.

Mid calf stretch I noticed a middle aged man who had appeared and started talking to us in a mix of Italian and English. He was keen to show us his fishing magazines that he had purchased. I was confused though as he had two copies of the same edition. He was very animated and wanted to show us what them and the pictures and stories that were covered.

After a few minutes of trying to be pleasant and listening to him, it was really starting to bore me but not wanting to be rude, I discreetly returned to my stretching. This left Paul to deal with the riveting conversation of fishing hooks and reels. He has so much more patience than I do but could sense that he too wanted to get away.

I didn't hang around waiting for Emma to stretch as I could smell something really good and followed a scent. Roo tracked me and both of us had our noses to the ground, heading in the direction of the estuary close by. I could hear the faint callings of my name to return but ignored these as this smell was way too good to resist. Sniffing frantically I reached the juicy bit that this scent had brought me to, only to find that this scent was in the form of some very large feet. In fact the feet were massive, they weren't human feet, they were pointy with very large claws on the ends of them.

Roo was barking as she came tearing towards me and she rarely barks so I wondered what the panic was. I turned to see her and she could see the huge feet too and was on her hind legs and going crazy, barking and growling.

My gaze took me from these huge feet up some very long and skinny legs then to a plump body that had feathers on it. I had never seen anything like this before or since and just then I saw it move. This made Roo go mad barking and howling constantly and warning me away from this thing. The foot moved again but this time in a kicking motion towards me, then again and again. Realising that this wasn't the friendliest of welcomes I turned and ran back to the beach to the safety of where Paul and Emma were.

I'm was still stretching and noticed that both dogs were racing towards us from the direction of the estuary, they looked panicked as if they had seen something that had unnerved them both. Paul was still being talked to death by the most boring person in this village about fishing and was clearly not picking up any signs that he was talking about something we know nothing about nor wanted to know about.

I couldn't calm the dogs down and they were racing backwards and forwards from the estuary then back to us on the beach. I walked to see what they were barking at and saw there was a very large Emu standing in a small pool of water in the estuary towering over all of the other ducks which in comparison made them look minute.

At first I thought it was a statue and was amazed to see it move. What on earth was an Emu doing in Italy in this small estuary? I ran back to the beach and confronted the boring guy pulling him away from his magazines and he confirmed that yes, it was an Emu. I later found out that this Emu had been donated by an Australian tourist a few years ago and now lived there and was quite tame. We headed back to Teddy via the Emu which looked so out of place there but it seemed to be happy enough.

It rained that evening and I love the sound of rain if I know it will be sunny the following morning. The four of us were all snuggled in the motorhome and the rain on the roof made us feel all snug inside. I closed all of the windows and we relaxed and kicked back, watched a movie and I made us hot chocolate with marshmallows. These were such happy times, as long as the rain doesn't turn to storms which as you know we've also experienced.

CHAPTER THIRTEEN

BELLISSIMO SAN ROCCO

Paul and I talked about and were planning our next place to stay which can be challenging at times, because there are so many options. Having had no recommendations from other fellow travellers about this area of Italy, the world really was our playground. We have the freedom to travel anywhere we want and we tend to base this on the sun and check weather forecasts before moving on. Our lessons learnt from our time in Croatia and the storms we had there still sit with us. We could have checked before heading there though part of me thinks that this was a one off freak storm.

The camper contact app downloaded onto our iPad is extremely useful as this showed us the sites in the area and Europe as a whole and you can filter your search on facilities needed, free spots or places close by and on this occasion it highlighted a spot on the west coast, only a two hour drive away called San Rocco.

We set our route on the ever unfaithful Connie to take us off toll roads and this took us through winding roads, up through the mountains and along the scenic roads of the Italian coast opening up some amazing vistas of the most fantastic views we've ever seen. Paul was driving so I was able to help him navigate through what was often hazardous bends with only single track lanes, blind bends plus constant erratic Italian drivers racing at top steed heading at us from all directions.

Throughout the whole of Europe we found the drivers in Italy to be far less considerate than other nationalities. The only rules they seem to observe, are to overtake on blind bends and to ignore the speed limit. They don't seem to have a brake pedal on their cars and have no patience at all when stopping to give way. If they have to pass you they don't make eye contact and they just drive onwards at full speed not giving you a second glance and it was as though being in a huge motorhome made us completely invisible.

The scooter drivers were even worse and were all obviously planning their own death on the roads as they weaved in and out in between the traffic as if it was a game and we've often had scooters on the wrong side of the road driving towards us and only swerving at the last minute just in time to miss us.

Whilst in Italy we saw a scooter driving school that was teaching learners how to drive them and an instructor was there showing the technicalities of how to steer and navigate around traffic cones in the car park. We watched them, wondering what the point was, because as soon as they get out onto the road they drive like maniacs. So very dangerous but amazingly we never saw any crashes or road accidents whilst in Italy.

We arrived in San Rocco where our stay was in a small car park with no facilities, just a stunning view of the small village Comogli. There were a few other motorhomers who had also parked up, mostly from the Netherlands and Germany and only us and one other motorhome from the UK. It was free to park here during the week and 15 euro per day at weekends so naturally we arrived midweek.

This area of Italy seemed a safe place, unlike the cities we visited, but regardless, we always take our passports and hide our laptops and iPads before heading out for a walk or run. I've heard a couple of stories of people being robbed when they leave their motorhome and I really couldn't be bothered with the hassle of having to find somewhere to get windows or doors fixed so feel happier if everything is out of sight before leaving Teddy unattended.

Another tip that we heard from other motorhomers is to leave a dog bowl outside of your motorhome as this often deters thieves, making them think there is a dog inside. A lot of motorhomers put signs on their windows with a picture of a vicious looking dog with a warning to beware. Our Labrador Roo has her own device that deters potential burglars. She likes to sleep in the front seat with her head resting on the steering wheel, obviously only when we are stationary. As her head becomes heavier from her sleeping this added pressure is enough to sound the horn. At first this used to make her jump, but now it is a regular occurrence and something she is used to happening now. It does sometime wake us through the night but as she has found the most cramped spot to sleep in at night then we guess she is happy there so don't want to move her.

This spot was perfect for us as there was adequate room for us to allow for the dogs to get out and safely have a sniff around. We soon got settled for the evening and Ozzie and Roo were due a walk so we set off on our way towards the small town close by. We arrived at a small palladium on the way which had fantastic views across the ocean and in the distance you could see Genova which is about twenty kilometres away.

Paul and I both said that it felt like walking onto a film set, as the sky, trees, and flowers were so beautifully coloured that they didn't look real and looked more like a backdrop you would see in a theatre production of Swan Lake. The air was filled with beautiful scents of honeysuckle and the olive groves around us created an eerie mist across the fields that made this place even more intriguing. It was just so amazing and hope I have managed to paint an accurate picture of this for you to imagine. If not then just go! Though I will add that the parking area is nothing special. To view the real beauty you need to be willing and able to lace up your walking shoes and get out and explore the surrounding area.

We walked on further and found some steps heading down and saw a middle aged couple making the ascent whilst desperately gagging for air, quite worryingly puffing and panting. I presumed that they must be fairly unfit and then understood why they looked exhausted as we started our descent of the 700 very steep steps which took us to Comogli. It's a seaside fishing village that was stunningly beautiful with small fishing boats dotted along the shore and bars and restaurants settling up tables and chairs in time for the evening rush.

We stopped for drinks at a small tavern and was offered what is another one of my favourite things in Italy, food. You usually get served aperitifs with all drinks and depending on the establishment these can be amazing. On this occasion they were a little disappointing with only a few olives, crisps and chilli crackers. However the aperitifs did not spoil my perceptions of the place as we sat and soaked up the atmosphere around us whilst psyching ourselves for the steep climb we had to get back to the motorhome.

We had stopped again and I could see that it was a bar and they were getting a drink. I rolled my eyes at Roo and knew we were going to be there for a while and I wanted to get back to those stairs, there was some cat food left out there and I wanted to finish it off before some other dog found it.

I strained on my lead and jumped to get Emma's attention but could see the glass in her hand and knew she wouldn't be disturbed. A small cracker hit my ear and fell to the ground which was supposed to keep me quiet. Which it did and the next few minutes went something like this. Jump, another cracker, jump, another cracker, delay, cute face, cracker and so on until I had devoured the full tray of crackers and we left.

Success, and our leads were unclipped from the cracker thrower also known as Emma which made Roo and I race off in the direction of the steps. We both knew about the cat food so this was a competition to see who got to it first. I raced as fast as my legs could take me but Roo was in the lead. I could smell the food was getting closer and I watched as Roo devoured it in one go. You can imagine I wasn't too pleased with her that evening and the silent treatment racked her with guilt as she constantly pestered me to apologise for her greed. It was my food to have after all not hers.

Ozzie and Roo raced up the stairs at a rate of knots and by the time Paul and I reached them they were both sitting at the top waiting for us, panting and out of breath, though I didn't know what the rush was all about. Back in the motorhome I fed Ozzie and Roo a belly full of their favourite food, tuna fish and dried biscuits fueling them for the walk we had planned the following day, not that any of us needed the exercise considering the stairs we had just climbed.

The following morning we woke up early, wide eyed and bushy tailed and set off for Portofino. We knew it was a challenging trek so we packed sandwiches and plenty of drinking water for us and the dogs and we hoped that water would also be available for filling our bottles on the route. The start of our walk was directly from the car park where we had stayed and involved the ascent of lots of steps. One thousand of these in fact, as I counted these as I found that this kept me focused to keep going.

Once we reached the top of the stairs we were exhausted and out of breath. Not surprisingly we were the only ones there and we were happy that the dogs were safe to be let off free from their lead to run and that we had tackled the hardest part of the walk. There is an alternative route you can take to Portofino via a lower path, but this is longer though not as steep. Alternatively you could just take a boat straight there but we like a challenge hence the reason we chose this route.

This is a gorgeous trek as it takes you to the top of the mountains and through forests and beautiful woodland eventually winding its way to the bay of Portofino. On the way you get tantalising glimpses of bays and beaches and there are numerous lookout points to stop off and take a breather.

Portofino was quiet as we had reached there early enough and before the tourists arrived from their cruise ship tours. It was 9am and the cafes and market stalls were just opening up in preparation for the crowds to spend their money. We had heard so much about Portofino and that it was a popular place to visit for its beauty and we weren't disappointed.

We sat in one of the cafes' close to the harbour and watched as the cruise ships entered the port and then tourists dismounted in their hundreds all eager to be there taking pictures and admiring the beautiful scenery.

What was such an idyllic and peaceful place only twenty minutes earlier turned into a bustling and chaotic small port. As mentioned earlier our advice is to visit places either early in the day or late at night once tourists have left. This way you see the real beauty of places and also get better photographs. Just as we did in Venice getting up and out earlier really pays off.

People watching from the café where we were sitting was fascinating, realising that all of the tourists that had left the cruise ship were all on the large side. I know that some cruises tend to be luxurious, offering guests copious amounts of food and alcohol to indulge themselves in an all-inclusive deal, basically eat as much as you want/can.

One of the tourists sat next to us and noticed that she was literally wedged in a small wicker chair, her body pouring over the sides, literally bursting out of her clothes and looking awfully uncomfortable with it. We had never seen such a large proportion of obese people in one place at any one time. I had an urge to jump from my seat, gather them all around to join me in an exercise class to burn some calories. My days of working as a personal trainer nearly kicked in and I wanted to do something to help these people and get them back in shape. I fantasised about grabbing the enormous crepe from one mouth and was internally pleading her to stop eating!

I did however restrain myself from doing this but feel that cruise ships should issue a warning in their terms and conditions before embarking on a long trip. Warning, "this cruise will dramatically affect your health and will result in you gaining excess weight of 50lbs".

We sipped our coffees and watched as the waiters around us were thrown into organised chaos by the arrival of so many tourists. We watched as they juggled orders, languages and dialects, an impressive skill and talent I thought. The teamwork between them was impressive and all customers were seated and served within minutes of arriving. This café was working like clockwork and this type of service and skill can often be difficult to find.

Ozzie and Roo sat next to us and were also enjoying the people watching. They were occasionally acknowledged by some of the dog loving tourists who asked them to pose with them for a picture. This happens a lot and always amuses us, especially when we go to places of real beauty and people still want a picture of our dogs. Look at the fantastic scenery and beautiful snow peaked mountains? But no they would rather have a photograph of a dog and no doubt they now appear on cameras and various holiday memories from all over the world.

I woke up after a good eight hours sleep but still felt exhausted with all the walking, running and exploring that we had done over the past few days. I needed a break from this but I sensed another walk coming as I saw Emma put her shoes on which meant we were off out again! She has got to be joking I thought to myself and surely we deserved a rest. Our leads clipped on and now it was certain that we were off out again.

My legs were tired and sore and in desperate need of a massage. Roo was tired too and I can always tell this as her cheek bones stand out and her eyes look glazed. We both needed to rest so I hoped we would just have a lazy day but these type of days never happen, not living with Paul and Emma anyway.

I stared at Emma with my big eyes and put my cutest expression on, willing her to sit down and stay in. It is times like this that I really wish I could talk to her. Standing outside in the warm air it smelt good and this instantly gave me a second wind. I glanced at Roo who always finds the energy to keep going, straining to be free from her lead and within seconds we found ourselves bursting with energy and racing through the long grass. We had been there for a few days so were familiar with the area and the smells around us.

The walking that we had completed in this area of Italy over the days we spent here was amazing. We covered many miles of this beautiful coastline and the walks were by far the most beautiful and well sign-posted that we'd done so far.

Frutuoso bay was our stop off point on another one of our walks and you could see this bay fast approaching us as we walked along the cliff edge. The views were stunning and we laughed as Paul and I commented that even Roo seemed to stop in her tracks for a moment to admire the view. It was clearly visible that the dogs were just loving their travels with us and all of the walks we had taken them on, their trails wagging like mad and I swear Ozzie actually smiled at us that morning!

This life is great and I'm exploring all these different places and tasting all of the different foods from bins from all over Europe. My life probably would have been the same old routine if we hadn't moved although I still do often think about Miffy and the dust she left behind.

When I was running through the beautiful wooded area I could smell food and saw Paul and Emma standing way too close to the cliffs edge. Wondering what on earth they were doing, they were just standing there. I approached them and twisted myself around their legs and jumped up to get their attention but they were distracted by something else.

This walk was long and strenuous and we took cheese and ham out for the dogs to keep them fuelled and this also kept them close to us and encouraged them not to run too far away. In particular Ozzie, as she will do almost anything for food and can smell the ham as soon as I take it from my pocket. Sometimes I don't even have to shout her name, she can just smell it and depending on her mood then comes running to me.

We continued walking in the direction of the bay and were greeted by crystal blue waters and an idyllic beach taken directly from my image of one of the most beautiful beaches in the world. Small cafes and restaurants were dotted along the beach and most sold grilled sardines or local fresh fish caught that morning. The smells oozing from these places was making our mouths water but our motorhome budget didn't allow us to be so extravagant so we sat on the beach and ate our cheese sandwiches that we had made earlier.

We spotted small fishing boats in the bay and the sun high in the sky reflected and shimmered on the shallow waters warming the water making it almost too tempting. Of course we took a dip to cool off and freshen from our walk, Ozzie only going as far to get her ankles wet. The water so clear the fish swam past us and this entertained Roo no end as she attempted to catch these.

This is the bay where Christ of the Abyss is submerged under the water. We wanted to view this so I asked a man who was standing near the small fishing boats and who seemed to be in charge of operating these. He spoke very good English and within seconds he let out a loud whistle and a small fishing boat appeared next to us.

Ozzie hopped straight onto the boat and was sitting there waiting whilst Roo totally freaked out, she just wouldn't get on. She was becoming really stressed and started to whimper and her body was shaking with fear. This wasn't a new mode of transport for her as she had been on boats before many times so we didn't understand why she was acting this way.

Roo was totally embarrassing as she wouldn't get onto the boat. I just got on with no problems at all whereas Roo had a tantrum and attracted unwanted attention from the other holiday makers there. It is usually me who is the wimp and I surprised myself actually as I'm not a big fan of these things either as they keep moving and the rocking doesn't stop and I have to remain on the same spot to balance myself.

Roo was causing such a commotion and lots of people were looking so eventually I lifted her onto the boat which made her roll into a small ball and as soon as the boat moved her tail wagged and she was relaxed again. If Roo thinks about things for too long she gets frightened so in some cases she has to be forced. Just like the time she wouldn't get onto the escalator in Hamburg and initially resisted it but once on she loved it, turning to want to try it again and go back down.

So eventually we were all in the boat and I turned to admire the scenery and to also have a good look at the half-naked Italian hunk who was kindly steering the boat for us. He took us out of the bay about 80 metres, stopped the boat and we glanced over and could see the figure of Christ in the water. We were given a huge telescope that he placed in the water and we took turns looking through it at this magnificent sight. Well, Paul and I did, Ozzie and Roo weren't interested.

Christ of the Abyss is a huge bronze monument under the water which was placed there in 1954 after a keen scuba diver Duilio Marcante was troubled by the death of one of his friends who had drowned off these shores. He wanted to promote a project and placed the sacred figure under the water as a symbol for divers to turn to in danger.

This statue is visited by thousands of people each year and we learnt that scuba diving is an expensive pastime in the bay and only allowed at certain times of the year.

I wanted to get off the boat, it rocked too much and my legs were sore with trying to keep a balance. Roo was by now quite happy and stretched herself out with her head looking over the edge at the fish swimming by.

I strained on my lead then eventually felt us moving again and gripped with my legs to stop myself from falling. Land was fast approaching and I barged past Roo and took a running leap from the boat onto the pavement yanking Paul with me as he still had hold of my lead.

As soon as I was back on land my lead was released and I was off and ran onto the beach. Roo didn't follow me this time she took another wobbler not wanting to get off the boat. As you can imagine I was shaking my head at her, she really is the biggest attention seeker and the crowds were again around her just smiling and admiring her which she just lapped up.

We had a long trek back to Teddy and thank goodness Emma had our water bowl and filled it with cool refreshing water that I dived into and quenched my thirst. Roo waited patiently and drank the remaining water that I had left for her. If you remember I only allow her to drink the water, once I have finished and never allow her to drink before me. She knows this is Ozzie's rule confirming that I am indeed the top dog.

Onwards we went and after stopping for a cool drink on our way back to Teddy the mountains of Frutuoso were quiet and we had the place to ourselves. There was a small restaurant on route that was also a B&B and would make a fantastic place to spend a night though the lack of access for vehicles would put many people off.

Once we got back to Teddy the dogs were hungry and an extra-large portion of food was on the menu for them that night. I had a tin of sardines for Ozzie and some chicken for Roo. After their meal their bellies were full and within moments they were sprawled out on the seats at the back of the motorhome and fell fast asleep.

Paul and I freshened up, made some pasta for tea, it was a beautiful clear night and we sat outside in the warm air and watched as the sun went down reflecting back on what had been a perfect day. We both agreed that it had been an amazing day, one of the best so far in fact, and soon the bottle of Valpolicella was empty and it was time for bed, we humans were exhausted too.

The following day was Friday. Before our travels on Friday nights Paul and I would go to our local pub the Moor House for a drink, eat crisps and talk about our week. The days between Monday to Friday meant we were like passing ships, not seeing much of each other and never having the opportunity to find out what we had both been up to. This Friday in Italy saw us sharing every moment of yet another day with each other and the dogs. We had nowhere to be and no one to answer to and we realised how much our lives had changed!

The dogs always came to the pub with us on Fridays and sat either side of us waiting for the odd crumb or snack to fall from the table. We love socialising but hadn't really had the chance to do this with travelling in a motorhome so we thought a night out was in order.

Whilst out walking we had met a couple who recommended a bar/restaurant next to where we were parked. I thought it was strange for Paul not too have sniffed this out until they explained that it was built into the cliff so was difficult to find.

The car park where we were staying, was busy with other motorhomers and as it was nearing the weekend there was a chilled atmosphere and good buzz in the air. People outside their motorhomes chatting, having BBQ's and drinking wine. I was looking forward to going out and after a shower, we put our best clothes on and decided whether to take or leave the dogs. As it was a busy place we didn't want to leave the dogs in case they disturbed our neighbours, so we took them, which later proved to be a big mistake.

Within five minutes of leaving Teddy we reached a small local bar where we had been for some food a couple of nights previous and the friendly owner poured us some wine and gave us a selection of aperitifs to sample. They were nice, small pieces of pate, and salami which were just delicious. Ozzie and Roo loved this place and spent their time sniffing around the bar area and picking up all of the scraps of food that had been left on the floor from other customers. This delighted the owner as it saved him from having to sweep these up so he was happy just to leave them to it.

We wandered on and found the hidden restaurant and it was literally set right into the rock with lots of coves and seats carved into the rock. When we arrived it was busy and the owner greeted us asking if we had a reservation. Not realising we had to make a reservation we apologised and said no. He confirmed that this was ok but that we may have to wait a while for a table.

We stood to one side and watched the people already in the restaurant and I noticed that the clientele looked sophisticated and well dressed and none of them had dogs.

Living in a motorhome does pose its limits with the cooking, cleaning and preening facilities but we didn't look too out of place and mingled with the locals outside waiting for our table. Both dogs had been sitting obediently next to us when I suddenly felt the lead in my hand jerk forwards and I heard the gasps from people around us.

I looked down at Roo and saw that she was vomiting, she had never been sick before so I was shocked to see this. She kept on spewing and spewing and it was going everywhere. By this time the crowds had moved well away from us and I tried to drag her away from the entrance but she was stuck to the spot and wouldn't move. Her stomach was convulsing and contracting with the outcome of sick, more sick and even more sick teaming out of her mouth.

Literally everyone's eyes were on us as Roo continued to take centre stage and the tutting and comments from the locals made us feel really embarrassed although I was more concerned about Roo.

Paul and I started to frantically try and pick the sick up using the poo bags that we had with us but the huge amount of sick meant we either needed a bin liner or better still a jet wash so this was an almost impossible task. We scraped up most of what we could into the bags and whilst we were doing this Ozzie decided the sick looked appetising and started eating the remains of this from the ground. Roo eventually started to come around and acted normal again and this is when Ozzie decided it was her turn to vomit. Just as violently and just as much. Both dogs would not move, no matter how much we yanked and pulled at their leads. Paul picked Ozzie up mid vomit and left her a few yards away to continue and then came back for Roo who by this time had started to eat the vomit Ozzie had just brought up.

This was so awful for the customers in the restaurant and we felt so bad for the owner. I went to see him and apologised and asked for some cleaning materials to try and make amends. He didn't speak at first and he didn't have to say anything. I knew by his facial expression that he was furious with us. He asked me to go which I did, apologising to the customers as we left.

We walked back to Teddy, our tails between our legs and we can only assume the dogs had eaten something that had disagreed with them, maybe something they had found on the floor from the previous bar we visited.

So our Friday big night out had fallen flat and lasted less than forty five minutes. Thankfully the gesture we offered the next morning to the owner of the restaurant of a bottle of wine was warmly accepted along with our groveling apology.

I was sick as a dog that night and it took me a while to recover. Each time Roo vomited I would eat this up, until I was sick and then Roo would eat it and this made her vomit again. Emma had to be quick and literally had to drag Roo away from the pile of vomit as this was making all of us ill.

Things just got worse for me as this is where I also got my head stuck in a fence. I wandered out for the afternoon and sniffed the area, some of the food was still on the barbeque left over from the other motorhomers that had been here so I stopped off for a chargrilled snack on my way to some more tempting smells.

There was an aroma of stale food in the air which I tracked down, having to poke my head through the small hole in the fence and managed to gobble most of it up. Even with my upset stomach nothing ever puts me off food and this tasted really good. I was eager to get more and pushed harder to get more food until I realised my head was stuck. I thought this was ok at first and someone would come and get me so I stood, head in fence and waited, and waited. I felt several sniffs at my bottom and hoped it was Roo and not some strange dog but being trapped in the fence I couldn't turn to see who it was.

I stood there for longer than I had initially imagined and was standing there head in fence for what felt like ages. It was getting cold and dark and I did start to get worried and wiggled a little more to try and break free. I tried it one more time and pushed backwards as hard as I could and twisted and wriggled and then eventually my head became free. Luckily still attached to my body but sadly without my collar which was left dangling on the fence. Goodness knows how long I had been there but hopefully no one will have missed me.

When I found Emma she noticed straight away that my collar was missing and asked me where it was and where I had been. Obviously I don't speak so I just looked at her and put my cute face on for a while which worked as I got a piece of ham and a cuddle. Being back in Teddy I couldn't stop thinking about the rest of the food that was on the other side of the fence that I couldn't quite reach. I saw an opportunity to escape and get this and managed to sneak away without anyone seeing me and lodging my head into the hole again.

I could see my collar was still there, exactly where I got stuck the last time. I wriggle my head through and stretched my tongue as far as I could to reach the food but this time I really got stuck. The food literally inches away, just within sniffing distance made it unbearable.

I yelped and then another yelp and another and eventually Paul found me still with my head stuck in the fence. He helped me to get free and he also retrieved my collar, picked me up and he dropped me back off back in Teddy. No ham or cuddles and I think he muttered that I should have learnt my lesson the last time really.

Paul found Ozzie with her head firmly wedged in a fence where she had escaped to. We realised she had done her disappearing act again and wasn't with us and after walking around where we were staying, we found her standing waiting patiently to be released from the fence!

She had obviously been there before as her collar was dangling on the other side of the fence next to where she was found. It took a few attempts for Paul to release her as she was well and truly wedged in and she was yelping to be released. In an attempt to break her free it was impossible so Paul had to break away some of the fence panels to get her out. We would like to think she wouldn't do this again but her stomach rules her head and if there is food involved she will do anything to get to it.

It was time to leave San Rocco and we headed off early Saturday morning, before the ticket inspector arrived at 8am and ventured north up the coast to a small coastal town near Cherasco. We took the toll road there as Connie indicated that it was 1h 30 on toll roads and nearly seven hours off them, we trusted her and this time we were right to do so. However we were expecting the worst and had plenty of money at the ready so we were surprised when we were only charged 7 euro to make the journey there. Paul worked out that we had probably saved that in diesel so sometimes toll roads have their uses.

We got to the campsite in good time, at around 10.30am after stocking up at a local supermarket called Euro spin where they sold very cheap produce. At the camping area we were greeted by the manager who was a very flamboyant Italian man in his early 30's. He was energetic and talked at high speed explaining the protocol to adhere to in the campsite.

He was high on life (or something else) and it was a real challenge to stop him from talking at us so we had no choice but to sit and listen. He told us all about his boxing career and educated us on the diet that all boxers should follow and the high protein chicken and fish that he has to eat each day.

He told us all about the meals he eats and the supplements he has to take to compliment his diet and exercise. This information would have been really useful to us if boxing was a sport we were looking to take up but unfortunately my slipped discs, aching knees and fear of getting my nose broken makes it a sport I don't wish to pursue.

Eventually I had to interrupt him as after sitting there at the entrance of the site for twenty minutes we were not even parked up. I don't even think he heard me speak. He was dressed in kaki camouflage combat trousers and a plain black vest top. Very much like the outfits Sylvester Stallone used to wear in his movies. Hence the nickname he instantly inherited, Rocky.

Paul and I again were patient and waited for a pause so we could get on the site but he continued to chat more about his boxing achievements. This was exhausting but he did eventually shut up.

I did the walk and found a spot, parked up and took our seats outside to have our lunch in the sunshine. Just then, Rocky appeared warning us not to use our camping table or chairs. He said we cannot act like campers as it is a car park zone as opposed to a campsite. I nodded, agreed, then took my chair back outside once he had disappeared. All the other motorhomers had their tables and chairs out so why couldn't we?

We found that most of the sites we have stayed at have different rules that are usually shown to you upon entering, usually on a board and not usually delivered to you in a presentation format by an eccentric Italian guy! Some people follow these rules and some don't.

It was around 14.30 when we heard another motorhome pull in and it was the English couple who had been parked next to us in San Rocco. Alan and Helen had taken the non-toll road route which shows the difference in times between the two routes.

Rocky was in his element at the arrival of new guests and we watched him as he demonstrated how he punched and ducked and dived to miss his opponents and then started to show them videos on his phone of himself competing in fights.

The English couple were subjected to Rocky's stories which pleased us as it kept him away from us so we continued with our lunch outside!

Hearing the conversation still going on in the background I overheard Alan mention Robson Greens name. Being from the North East I know Robson Green is something of a celebrity. Rocky rushed to our motorhome to look at Paul exclaiming "mucho celebrity, are you famous and rich?" We didn't realise at first that he was implying that Paul was in fact Robson Green. I used to walk the dogs with Robson's uncle in Wideopen but failed to see the resemblance here. Rocky was unbelievably excited by this point and was staring at Paul and looking really impressed that there was a celebrity actually staying at his place, but don't call it a campsite.

I didn't even bother trying to explain that Paul was Paul and not Robson Green as this would really start to get into a lengthy conversation. To be honest I had had enough of his stories and chatter for one day and escaped to sit inside with our chairs and our lunch, just how Rocky had initially wanted it to be.

Listening to Rocky's chatter throughout the day was very entertaining as most of the time he called his guests 'simple'. "Yes you are very simple". We were laughing at this point and I asked him later that day what he meant by this and he explained that it was because people from Great Britain do not cause any problems for him and that's why we are simple.

Throughout the next couple of days staying there we dodged him as much as we could because as soon as he caught sight of you he was there talking to you nonstop or wanting to see Paul again aka Robson Green. To be fair Rocky was a lovely guy, he made us feel very welcome and we departed wishing him all the luck in the world for his career in sport.

CHAPTER FOURTEEN

TEDDY GETS ILL

We arrived early evening at Villa Nova D'Asti which looked a nice aire, costing us 8 euro a night, for water, electricity but no Wi-Fi. It seemed a very quiet place, quaint and we were the only people there. It had been a long drive today and we were ready to stop, rest, have some food and relax.

After the egg test we realised we had parked slightly on a slope which made it challenging to prepare our evening meal as the chopping board and onions slid from the bench onto the floor. Both dogs investigated keenly and as usual were willing to get any additional morsel of food no matter how small. To get Teddy level, the chucks were needed and Paul placed them at the front wheels and drove onto them whilst I held the pan of boiling water filled with pasta. Which by the way is not recommended!

Everything was now in place and Teddy was level, though Paul had noticed a warning light appear on the dashboard and so attempted to start the engine again to investigate, only to find there was no life in Teddy's engine. No lights, no engine noise, nothing, apart from a clicking noise when the key was turned. It seemed as if Teddy had taken his last breath whilst driving onto the leveler. Teddy had really done it this time and his sudden death brought nothing but sheer frustration and disappointment. Though to be honest at first this didn't worry us as we are both pretty laid back so we thought it best to give it fifteen minutes then try again.

We ate our pasta, tried the engine again with the same result, nothing. We waited another five minutes to try again and still nothing. Ok, now was the time to worry as tomorrow we had to be in Turin. I was meeting a friend from the UK and we still had a fifty kilometre drive ahead of us.

Help wasn't at hand as we were the only motorhome in the camping spot and as we drove in we had noticed that the village around us was desolate with no sign of life to be seen and the streets and shops were all deserted. Close to the motorhome area I saw some lights in a large building and we headed there in the hope to find somebody who could help.

It was a local football club and as we entering the lounge area we were greeted by a large group of men, all with big red smiley faces. Whilst the weather had been hot this redness wasn't through sunburn and we guessed that this was something to do with the alcohol consumption judging from all the empty wine bottles on the tables around them.

The gentlemen were all very welcoming, friendly and were all absolutely plastered. I noticed a twinkle in Paul's eye and I knew he was looking for where he could sign up to join this club. His love of football and drinking suggested this would be a perfect combination for him.

As soon as we spoke their faces fell and they all looked puzzled, looking at each other and trying to work out what on earth we were saying. I did think to myself surely one of these red faced merry gentlemen must be able to speak a little English or even better be a mechanic though I am known as ever the optimist.

My attempt to speak Italian didn't help either until one guy shouted up I can speak English. Great I thought and I replied slowly, "we need a mechanic", followed by his reply which was, "I don't understand!"

He was no help so we moved to the bar area where I recognised a man there who had opened the gates for the motorhome area earlier that evening. He also didn't speak a word of English so I got his attention by carrying out a mime of us trying to start the motorhome and then collapsing to the ground and pretending to die! He nodded and said "ah mechanic." "Yes, yes" I cried and he got his phone out of his pocket and made a call.

My heart was in my mouth as I watched him talking and I was desperately trying to decipher any of the words he was saying. After the call he confirmed to us that at 8am tomorrow there will be a mechanic. I felt happier that help way on its way, though the promise of a mechanic at 8am on a Monday morning is one thing. Actually turning up is another.

Not wanting to appear unsociable we stayed at the bar as it was filled with the most delicious looking cakes and I had to have some. They were all home baked, with icing and fruit fillings and my weakness for cakes resulted in me working my way through a good few slices, with even the bartender looking astonished as to how much I could eat. By chance my Italian dialect stretches to being able to ask for more cake which came is useful here, piu torta per favour!

Paul was loving this place, with male company and a bar that sold large glasses of wine for 1 euro. He was making the most of this and was sampling the vino (which came out of a ten litre box behind the bar) and we tried our best to chat to the locals. It was a loud lively atmospheric bar and we both enjoyed watching them as they shouted and joked with one another and even though we didn't speak the same language we ended up having a great night with them all.

The following morning we woke early and we were eager for the arrival of the mechanic at 8am and by 8.10 we had started to get agitated and worried, my friend in Turin would be waiting for me and I didn't want to let her down.

Just then we heard a car in the distance that seemed to be getting closer and the sound of the engine was getting louder and louder until it reached the gates and hooray the mechanic arrived.

He was a very smart middle aged man driving a worn out knackered, rusty and battered old car that looked like it had just been rescued from the local tip and could disintegrate at any moment. In fact it looked like it needed a mechanic too.

He was very keen to get started and after a quick gesture of good morning he jumped straight into the front seat of the motorhome only to be confronted by Roo who wasn't happy with an intruder in her space. As soon as she clapped eyes on this person she didn't recognise she let out a loud gruff bark! I've never seen anyone move so fast, as this startled him so much that he leapt out of the seat and ran back to his car. It turned out that he hates dogs and was terrified of them. He wouldn't get out his car, so we secured both dogs away from the motorhome and reasoned with him to get out of his car again.

Eventually he plucked up the courage to leave his place of refuge and came and lifted the bonnet of Teddy and simply tightened something which made the engine fire up. We were delighted and had cash for him but he didn't charge us anything and wouldn't take it from us. He wrote something on a piece of paper, which translated, meant a lead on the starter motor was loose and would need replacing. Desperate now to get to Turin we thought that this could wait and all we needed to do was keep Teddy moving or make sure we parked on a downhill slope so we could push him should he breakdown again.

We arrived in Turin on time and had a lovely reunion with my friend Nellie, who was the same friend that had helped us a few weeks ago with the translation for the motor mechanic when we broke down. Seeing her again was lovely and it was also the first familiar face we had seen in ages with being away from home for so long. The gifts of maltesers, hair dye and my favourite magazines made it feel just like Christmas and this was certainly a highlight of my trip.

Nellie used to live in Turin and knew the area well so our first stop was a local coffee shop close to the hotel where she was staying. The café was full of local people and the noise of their chatter was deafening, with most seats taken, though we managed to squeeze into a corner next to the cake display which pleased me no end. Though my previous fix was only yesterday the sight of these cakes left my mouth watering and I was desperate to try some of the cakes which I did.

Ozzie and Roo were sitting next to me drooling in the hope of getting a piece of the cake and as usual they succeeded as the tiramisu looked nicer than it tasted so Ozzie and Roo got most of this. I was chatting and catching up with Nellie whilst keeping an eye on Roo and I was patting her head to comfort her as she waited for me to feed her more when I noticed her fur felt gritty, like she had sand in her coat.

I looked down and saw she had small black grains covering her head, her snout, and on closer inspection her whole body. We paid and left the café immediately and outside upon closer inspection my fears were confirmed, yes Roo had fleas. Making matters worse Ozzie had them too!

Ozzie and Roo had never had fleas before as the treatment I give them every 6 months prevents these. Even now, recalling this event and talking about these fleas makes me itch as there were literally thousands of them possibly millions covering both dogs. You could now see them quite clearly even without parting their fur.

Nellie accompanied us to the local vet who gave us something to treat them that they guaranteed would work. Some twelve hours after administering the medication I was disappointed to find that they were still there and the following morning we found that they had multiplied. Removing these turned into a mammoth task as the only option we had was to painstakingly remove these with a flea comb. I also had Teddy to fumigate as they were all over the motorhome and our laundry bills multiplied by the day as countless blankets, throws and bedding needed a thorough boil wash to eradicate these mites.

I didn't know what all the fuss was about. Emma didn't leave me alone and was constantly brushing me and checking my fur. I had to sit still whilst she used a special comb to brush my coat and then washed me twice. She had to force me in as I was not happy having to go in the shower for a second time. She was doing the same to Roo and was brushing us both for hours and hours. I looked at Emma willing her to stop but she continued to brush and brush us for what lasted most of that day.

After a thorough cleanse of both dogs, the motorhome and ourselves I was confident that we had managed to get rid the fleas so we could now move on and continue onwards.

Our next stop took us across the border into France. The N94 road that took us there was a scenic route that weaved through valleys, ski resorts, steep gorges and open land allowing us to see miles across the landscape. We finally stopped in Savines-le-Lac, a small scenic town surrounded by the natural beauty of the Alps.

Our home for the night was in a car park that had electricity supply, water and toilet dumping facilities. It was free so we liked it! The next morning we woke early and saw the sun coming over the mountains which made the colours of the trees stand out and the different rock formations surrounding them looked amazing.

Raring to get out and explore we got ready, made some sandwiches and headed out. We wanted to explore the area though we were aware that we still needed to find a garage that would be open and able to fix Teddy. Since leaving Italy, Teddy had been very temperamental, with Paul turning the key and not knowing if it would start or not. Sometimes it started and other times it didn't and this caused us to become a little anxious realising we really had to get this seen to.

We had learned to live with things like the motorhome not starting and always managed to get help at places where needed along the way. People are all too kind to help when they see others in need and there really are some lovely people in this world. We could of course have helped ourselves a little more and could have booked into a garage straight away but as Teddy was still working we tried to get a little bit more out of him before he finally gave up.

I was straining and really pulling on my lead. I wanted to be free and run as fast as my legs would take me. There were some amazing smells in this place and I needed to go and seek then out. Roo and I twisted and turned and changed direction until eventually I heard the clink of my lead being released and we were free running off into the distance. I sprinted ahead and I could hear Roo's footsteps pattering behind me. She was running much slower than me and I was outrunning her quite easily. It was clearly annoying her as I could see her trying to catch up as I glanced back mid sprint to see her striding out to try and catch me.

My nose was to the ground and I was sniffing every inch of this place. There was no food as yet but I sniffed in hope to find something to eat. I saw some water up ahead and had the dreaded feeling that I might actually have to get wet. We reached the water and Roo was of course straight in. I managed to skirt around the edges and only got the tips of my paws in and made it to the other side without any mishaps thank goodness as I didn't want a repeat episode of nearly drowning again.

Once clear of the water my nose led me to a large wooded area where my senses went wild and my tail was erect in the air as I could smell food. I tracked these smells and found myself in thick dense weed where success was in the form of some food which I ate as quickly as I could as Roo was on her way to get some too.

Stale bread is not the best of bush foods but the crusty bits tasted really good. I devoured it, every last morsel and then headed off to my next port of call, the rubbish bin which I dived into head first. It was the perfect height for me to be able to jump into and sniff out anything that was tasty in there. More smells and more food to be found, I saw some long grass and got amongst it and instantly felt a sensation of discomfort on my stomach and then it moved to my tail, then my head and at first I ignored this and continued to run onwards.

The sensation was getting intense and I felt a sharp needle sting me on my head and I felt a rush of pain in my stomach. The stabbing of sharp needles just kept happening but this time all over my body in particular on and around my stomach. I raced to find Paul and Emma and by this time I realised I was in pain and I did actually cry with the discomfort.

Wasps were surrounding and following me and I realised it was these that were sticking their needles into me and this hurt. I was howling for help and Roo came to see what was wrong, saw me covered in wasps and then raced off into the distance away from me.

During our walk, we were still looking for a garage when we heard the yelps of Ozzie and then saw her tearing toward us. She was hysterical and crying and looked uncomfortable and as she reached us we instantly saw what was causing this.

From head to tail she was swarmed by wasps, all covering her body and they were following her and stinging as she rolled in the grass to get them off her. She couldn't stand still as they were literally diving at her and stinging her furiously more and more continuing to return for another attack. Paul and I helped to swat these away without being stung but they were annoyed and more and more just kept appearing.

You could see in her face that she couldn't bear it any longer and raced off into the distance howling in agony, the howls became fainter and more distant as she continued to sprint off away from us. Paul, Roo and I had no choice but to chase after her to find her and eventually spotted her as a small dot on the horizon, no matter how fast we ran there was no catching her.

It seemed to take ages but eventually we caught up and were reunited. Ozzie was slumped by a small bench and was panting furiously, her tongue dangling from her mouth, she looked exhausted. Luckily she had managed to out run the wasps and was licking her wounds, her eyes were dazed and she looked very sorry for herself.

We gave her some water and Paul checked her over to see what damage the wasps had done and before our eyes we watched as a lump started to appear on the top of her head. The lump was growing and getting bigger and bigger and we noticed that one of the stings was still stuck in her head. The lump grew and grew and I could only think that this had given her an allergic reaction.

After what was such an eventful walk for Ozzie we decide to put the garage search on hold and starting heading back to Teddy to check her out properly, give her some rest and an antihistamine for the swelling on her head. On our way back Ozzie stayed really close to us which rarely happens and I think this may have given her a real fright and that she needed us for security.

Roo as ever was still full of life, raring to go and we watched as she raced ahead to greet another dog, a huge grey Bullmastiff that got one whiff of her, literally went mad and started chasing her. The expression on her face was quite a picture! Her eyes went huge and her ears pinned back as she raced away from it, running at top speed heading off in the opposite direction with the Bullmastiff chasing her closely behind.

I also panicked and wanted to save her without really wanting to get involved but she was running way too fast for me to help her. A woman appeared next to us with a lead, looking upset and waving her arms to indicate and warn us that her dog could bite and is mucho vicious!

Just then Roo raced past us, still followed closely by the very large aggressive Bullmastiff, the one we now knew bites other dogs! They were both running at full speed and I could see Roo was in a blind panic trying to get this dog away from her. Her eyes bulging, her tongue dangling as we watched her duck and dive and change direction to try and outwit the dog. As the Bullmastiff raced past us the lady managed to grab its collar which sent her flying across the path. It was a huge beast and she had to use all her strength to stop it in its tracks.

It wasn't happy! Its hackles were raised and it gave out a loud gruff bark as we maneuvered ourselves past it. Ozzie was terrified and was practically climbing on my back to get away from it. Goodness know why this woman had let the dog from its lead in the first place and I couldn't think how she managed to deal with its strength and size. Poor Roo was exhausted and limping next to us and looking at her I could see the relief in her face that she managed to get away without a scrape.

We continued home with a very badly stung Beagle who now looked like she had two heads, as the lump continued to grow. An exhausted Labrador, her legs squatted low to the ground, her eyes dark and dull and blood pouring from her paws from the cuts she had endured during her chase and Paul and I mentally exhausted by what had just occurred.

Once back at the safety of the motorhome Roo collapsed on her favourite seat and slept whilst Ozzie still whimpered in pain but thankfully allowed us to see her wounds. The lump on her head seemed to have stopped growing but looked painfully sore.

As she rolled onto her back she showed us hundreds of stings, all bright red blisters covered her freckly tummy. I checked all of the stings and treated them with antiseptic, then gave her an antihistamine and some of her favourite food, tuna fish, to make her feel better. That was enough to calm her down and after enough fussing decided she'd had enough of me and wanted her own time. Pushing me away with her paw, and then continued to lick off all of the cream I had just spent hours applying. She was happy, she obviously liked the taste and she had a lovely white tongue afterwards to prove it.

I had the most awful experience, worse than the pain from the excessive brushing last week and I was so uncomfortable and couldn't bear the awful feeling of the stinging. My belly was red with blisters and I had been stung many times which were all extremely sore. I had a new asset to add to my good looks too in the form of a very large lump on my head which wobbled when I moved it. The lump was so big I could see it if I strained my eyes upwards or if I caught my reflection I had to look twice as I didn't even recognise myself. I've told you about my looks, or lack of them, and you know that I am no dog model and not blessed with good looks at all but this lump only added to my unusual features. Forever in my shadow, my beautiful sister Roo was sound asleep next to me and even when I whimpered in pain she still didn't wake.

The next morning with both dogs still exhausted from the previous days' escapades and with us unable to find a garage in Savines-le-Lac we left, well, we tried to leave! I say tried as we now had a flat tyre that had been troubling us for some time now, but regular trips to the garage and top ups of air had got us by for a few weeks. It was however, now flat as a pancake but on the up side Teddy actually started up this time and the engine was roaring. However this only lasted for about three metres then the engine stopped! Deciding to try a bump start, I got out and started to push whilst Paul steered. After a feeble attempt I realised my lack of strength meant that I couldn't push it myself and we needed help.

Luckily there were some other motorhomers next to us and they came to offer help as they had been watching us struggle. Bearing in mind the two men looked a little fragile being in their late 70's with huge beer bellies and bright red faces, I instructed them to be careful. Normally I would have told them not to bother, but we needed help and they did offer. As we pushed I glanced behind me and saw the men pushing with all of the strength, with their bulging red faces and they were puffing and panting. My flip flops weren't giving me much support on the wet tarmac as by this time the heavens had opened and we were all getting soaked but in the midst of sheer frustration Teddy's engine kicked in and started and we were off. Flat tyre and all. We slowly drove away after giving our thanks, some wine and hugs to the two men that helped us and I was pleased to see that both men were both ok and fully recovered from the push they had given us.

We managed to get Teddy to the nearest garage and as we dared not turn the engine off again, we filled the tyre with some air which was a relief as driving any distance with a flat tyre can be incredibly slow and also damaging to the wheel if driven for long distances.

Connie informed us that there were garages in the town of Briancon so we headed there visiting numerous garages on the way. In fact, we visited nine garages in total with Paul waiting outside with the engine still running whilst I ran in and asked if they would be able to fix it for us.

This day stands out as one of the most frustrating as none of the garages I enquired within showed any sign of wanting to help. I used my French phrase book to help, asking the numerous mechanics for help. Excuses ranged from just a straight forward no, with no reasoning why, to we don't do motorhomes though the best excuse was no I cannot go outside it is raining!

Garage number nine was looming in the distance and it was at this point that my chin was starting to wobble. With tears forming in my eyes I wandered into the garage where a very kind mechanic looked at Teddy and confirmed that the starter motor was in need of a replacement and he could order the part and fix it. As he promised, this was fixed the following morning, along with a new tyre and despite the hefty payment we felt happy that Teddy was better again.

The 17th of October 2014 marked the 100th day of our travels in the motorhome and we went off in search of some atmosphere and life to celebrate this milestone. Being from Newcastle we are used to partying and socialising and at times travelling in a motorhome with two dogs had really restricted us from doing this as often as we are accustomed to. I hadn't worn make up nor a pair of high heeled shoes for 100 days and I wanted to go out, all dressed up and celebrate this day, any excuse really!

We looked on the map and the nearest town was Narbonne and looked like a fairly large town with plenty to do. This was music to our ears! Surely a large town must means cafes, bars, restaurants and some night life. We had kept a bottle of champagne chilling in the fridge since leaving the UK to mark this occasion and we were excited at the prospect of popping this and starting the celebrations.

We parked up and headed out with the dogs to find some life. It was such a pretty place with the canal du midi running through the centre of the town with beautiful flowers and bridges framing it as you walked along the pathway. There was a huge church and some beautiful architectural in the buildings surrounding the town square and spotted a restaurant sign so we made a beeline for it, though unfortunately there were no customers and no atmosphere there so we left without even buying a drink.

We walked the streets in search of somewhere suitable until Paul spotted an Australian bar that was on the other side of the canal called Cafe Walla Beer. We love Australia and anything linked to Australia, and we were excited at the thought of a VB or some Coopers Pale Ale.

A French chap greeted us as he sipped his vino at the bar and a group of young guys at a table near the back of the bar were playing cards. We ordered our drinks served by another French guy and soon came to the realisation that the name of the bar was the only resemblance to Australia. The beer was French and it was the only bar we have been to where the pumps contain more non-alcoholic drinks than alcoholic drinks. I believe there was water, soda water, lemon, coca cola, fanta and lemonade all on draft!

We stayed for a few more drinks in the hope that the party would start, the music would come on and Coopers Pale Ale would appear in the fridge. This didn't happen and we soon accepted the fact that there was no party happening in this bar and possibly not in this town! Slightly disheartened we walked home back to Teddy opened our bottle of Taittinger and prepared some cheese, olives, pate and crackers to accompany it. We clinked our glasses to toast the 100th day and sipped our champagne which was delicious and we commented that life was good.

Sitting outside of Teddy to catch the sunset we spotted a light on in the motorhome next to us. It was only 8pm and there was still plenty of champagne left, and I thought that our French neighbours may like some too. Paul shook his head as he was quite content in his own company but I was desperate to socialise and to create a party.

I knocked on their door and shouted "Bonjour, we have champagne would you like some?" An elderly gentleman answered the door in his dressing gown and I showed him the champagne asking if he wanted a drink. He looked confused at first and I filled a glass handing it to him. He accepted and said his wife was sleeping just as she appeared behind him in her nightdress.

Another couple walked past and I asked them to join us for a drink too. So, after I had managed to rally the troops, we had a party of six standing outside our motorhome, drinking champagne and we raised our glasses to good health and happiness. It turned out that the French gentleman was 76 and he and his wife had travelled for many years in their motorhome. He looked younger than his age and his wife who was standing next to me seemed a shy lady and was still wearing her night dress, not saying a word, with a look of total exhaustion and confusion on her face. To be honest, she didn't look too thrilled to be there.

The other couple were from Holland who had also been travelling for months around Europe and during conversation asked us what we missed most from the UK, apart from the obvious which were our family and friends.

My reply was Heinz baked beans as I love these and hadn't had a tin for over one hundred days. Stocking up on things like this was something we should have done before leaving England. This however ended up being the wrong thing to say as this lead to a very lengthy discussion on where to get beans in Europe. He explained you can purchase any kind of bean in Europe and he talked about the history of beans, the transportation, manufacturing and price and clearly far too much time on his hands to carry out his research on beans. He continued to talk and talk even more about beans and I was desperately looking for a way out of this. I was becoming increasingly bored and I stared at him in a trance in the hope he would stop talking which he didn't until I interrupted his lecture by filling his glass and raising this for a cheers to beans which thankfully worked.

Paul and Emma had friends around tonight and one of the men was so boring that he actually sent me to sleep, I was astonished as to how anyone could talk for so long about a bean. At first I was interested as it involved food, but after an hour I knew everything I wanted to know about beans and stopped listening and my boredom soon drifted me off into my snooze.

So no party that night but we did have some nice champagne, and also gained extensive knowledge about beans in Europe. Later that evening we ate chicken stew that had been in the slow cooker for hours, it was delicious and thankfully not a bean in sight.

CHAPTER FIFTEEN

KIDNAPPED IN PALAMOS

From Narbonne we travelled south and crossed the border into Spain and were surprised to see the roads frequented by plastic seats occupied by many prostitutes. We'd seen similar sights in Italy but never on a scale like this. Despite us thinking that a motorhome was the ideal mode of transport to entertain this industry we drove past without stopping, though Paul did seem to slow down for some reason.

Figueres was our first stop in Spain. A free stop at Castel de Sant Ferran provided a nice place to spend an evening, though more recent reviews have mentioned break-ins and groups of youths loitering at evenings. It was only a ten minute walk into town so we wandered in for Wi-Fi, a quick drink and a chance to practice our Spanish. Figueres is the home town of Salvador Dali and offers a museum, theatre and crypt, underneath which he is buried. As usual there were no dogs allowed in these attractions and we didn't want to leave the dogs alone in Teddy so we passed the chance to visit the museum and added it to our things list to come back for.

We climbed a very short hill the next morning towards Castel de Sant Ferran and set off to run around the path surrounding the remains. At exactly 3 kilometres this was a perfect run and provided lovely views of the surrounding areas and after a couple of laps the dogs and I returned to Teddy whilst Paul continued doing loops and loops.

All exercised and refreshed we set off, with Palamos picked out on the map. A new motorhome area was receiving good reviews and as it was just under an hour away, we were looking forward to a short and easy drive.

The motorhome area was as good as the reviews suggested and Empordarea remains one of the best places we have stayed at. It's situated just a ten minute walk to the centre which boasts dozens of bars and restaurants. We sampled a few of these before deciding that our favourite was the Casa Del Mar who offered an excellent menu del dia for only 10 euro per person to include bread, three delicious courses and a bottle of wine to share between two. You pay for the wine whether you drink it or not as Paul found to his cost during one visit.

Empordarea has all the necessary services available, such as water, dumping stations, showers, Wi-Fi and laundry. All for around 10 euro per night. The owners also rent out bikes, a convertible car and motorhomes. The staff are all very friendly, speak excellent English and all of these qualities meant we stayed here for over seven weeks which was our longest stop since leaving the UK.

We instantly felt at home and loved the surrounding area, in particular the hills and excellent running tracks that were behind the site. We spent hours running in the hills as the tracks went on for miles and miles through vineyards, wooded areas, walking trails, and best of all no traffic. A perfect spot for keen runners or walkers and the dogs loved being off the lead for the entire walk.

The beach was only a ten minute walk away and its golden sands stretched out along the coastline for as far as the eye could see. The water was warm and shallow so ideal for swimming which

Roo took advantage of on every visit. We found fantastic coastline walks both north and south of Palamos and enjoyed day after day exploring the paths and secluded beaches. Alongside walking and running our days in Palamos were filled with glorious sunshine and great local foods. Most evenings we spent at the beach, beer in hand as we watched the sun go down which we never grew tired of. It was November and the skies at this time of year were beautiful and perfect as one of my happy things in life is to see the clouds turn pink as the sun sets for the day.

On one particular evening there was a huge cruise ship leaving the port and it was lit up with hundreds of fairy lights. We watched as the ship sailed towards the horizon and could still hear the faint noise of chatter and music still going on in the distance.

The pink clouds turned to grey and before the night sky turned dark we headed towards the site and stopped off at a small traditional tapas bar that looked inviting. We always prefer to eat and drink at the local watering holes as you get to appreciate the area more, understand their way of life and also to brush up on our language skills. We took a seat at the corner of the bar so the dogs were out of the way, ordered wine and were presented with some freshly fried sardines and aioli, just delicious, and all free with your drink. We adore tapas and in such a short time have grown very fond of Spain and the Spanish lifestyle. The sun shines, the people are welcoming and friendly and certainly know how to rustle up the most delicious of dishes.

After great fun playing and walking on the beach we had ended up at another tapas bar. I found myself looking at Roo and was rolling my eyes with sheer disappointment as I thought we were heading home for our food. It was way past our dinner time though we did have a late breakfast as our run this morning was extra-long. I got comfy as I sensed we were going to be here for a while. I kept one eye open as I do like tapas and Emma always shares with us, my favourite being the anchovies. After a while I was getting bored and stretched up and clawed at Emma's legs for her to acknowledge me and take us home. She was too busy and was engrossed in a conversation with a Spanish woman. She sometimes talks in a different language and when she does this I have not got a clue what she is saying!

I was getting hungry now as the tapas had been quite sparse and I wanted some food so again I clawed and stretched up as high as I could, to get Emma or Paul's attention. Eventually I felt my lead being moved and we headed out into the cool night on our way back to Teddy.

I was starving and couldn't wait to get my dinner and I also needed to pee pee. Once we reached the field Paul released my lead and I ran into the bushes and was distracted by a delicious piece of pizza that had been discarded under a tree which I sniffed out and devoured in one go.

My nose was fixed on this small area and I looked for more food ignoring the calls that I could hear instructing me to return. I was successful in my search as I found more food and it was delicious. I ate every last bit and then dashed out to catch up with Paul and Emma who weren't there and my first thought was, that they were hiding. They were not there! I couldn't hear them calling and didn't know what direction they had went. I was all alone and didn't feel so tough or confident anymore. My anxiety had started and the all too familiar knot in my stomach was there. I stood and howled for them to hear me but there was no reply. It was dark, I was cold and scared and I wanted my Paul.

Quickly thinking through my options I decided to go back to the tapas bar we had just left and darted across the grass through all of the bushes and ran straight across the busy road out of sheer desperation to find them. I heard a screeching of brakes and bright lights dazzled my vision. I heard a man shouting at me from his car though thankfully it was in Spanish so I didn't understand. I raced into the tapas bar and sniffed where we had been just a few moments ago but the seats were empty, no Emma, no Paul and no Roo.

I went outside and started really panicking and howled and howled, praying that they would hear me. My anxiety took its full force and I was salivating and being sick bringing up the contents of the food that I had just devoured in the bush.

I was shaking uncontrollably, my body was stiff with worry and couldn't move as I didn't really know where I was and also didn't know which direction home was. Lots of people appeared next to me and they were all looking at me and speaking using different words which again I didn't understand.

I felt the warmth of a hand picking me up and lifting my head I came face to face with a strange looking man. In fact I had never seen another human look like this before. He had colourful skin like it had a painting on it and rings in his ears and nose. His eyes were dark and dull with no life or sparkle to them and he clumsily lost his grip of me sending me crashing to the floor. I whimpered and cried, desperately wanting to be back with my family, Paul, Emma and Roo.

I had a glimmer of hope when I felt a tug on my neck and turn in the hope of seeing Paul's face but no it was the strange looking man again and he had put me on a lead. I knew then that there was no way of getting away. I stared at him pleading with him to unclip the lead but his dull eyes made no contact with mine.

I sniffed the lead attached to me and knew it definitely wasn't mine in fact it was awful and smelt terrible. I wriggled for it to be released but it was fastened tight and I couldn't get this off me.

Next thing I know I was taken outside and into a small car and although I was reluctant to get in and I pulled back on the lead, I was lifted and thrown onto the back seat which was a poor start as my usual place on the front seat.

After a long journey of twists and turns the car stopped and my hopes of being reunited with my family were dashed as we were parked outside a house, in fact a very small house. Again I was dragged by the lead and I was reluctant to enter but I found myself picked up by the weird looking man and placed this time on a small very damp sofa in what was a dark and very smoke filled room.

I couldn't see my paw in front of my face it was so smoky. It wasn't until a few moments later that I realised there was another very strange looking man on the sofa next to me. He spoke to me but his language wasn't familiar, in fact nothing he said registered. He unclipped my lead and I immediately dived from the sofa to search for the door to try and get out of this place. The door we had entered through was closed and this disappointment made me howl and cry even more.

I stood by the door in the hope it would open but no matter how much I cried, it remained closed. I was now feeling tired and no matter how hard I tried to stay awake my eyes started to close. I tried to keep them open but they continued to close and I fell into a deep, deep sleep in an almost unconscious state.

I was woken up to a very loud noise which made me jump and for a moment I thought I was back home in Teddy but no, I was still in this damp and smoky place.

Whatever the noise was that had woken me didn't bother me again as I felt sleepy and could see clouds of smoke drifting across the room. My eyes felt heavy and I had to fight to stay awake but in no time I was asleep again only this time I had the weirdest of dreams.

Roo and were flying and we were high up in the sky bouncing off the clouds and we both couldn't stop wagging our tails. Roo wagged hers so much that it fell off and then miraculously another tail grew and this happened time and time again. The sky in my dream was a deep purple colour and there were parrots and elephants flying with us.

I drifted in and out of sleep and was abruptly woken mid dream just as Roo's tail had dropped off again and I felt a heavy weight on my body. It was the smelly guy who seems to have the same problem as me, trying to stay awake and he had actually crashed out on top of me on the floor still next to the door which still hadn't opened. I can honestly say that I had never smelt *this odour before. I was stuck, my body just wouldn't move no matter how I tried. Stay awake I told myself, get out of this place I said but again I fell into a sound and deep sleep again.*

I knew that this excessive sleeping was not normal, I like sleeping but this was taking it too far. Luckily when I woke the smelly guys had moved away from me but the smell was lingering. As I woke I could see it was the morning as light was coming in through the window and to this day I could have sworn I saw Roo flying past, I was however very bleary eyed and was surprisingly exhausted even after my marathon sleep.

After a few seconds of realising that I was not dreaming and I was actually awake and my anxiety started to increase, my stomach cramps were painful and then my uncontrollable salivation started. My whole body was tense and I just wanted to go be back with my family.

I couldn't move I was stuck to the spot, rigid exhausted and incredibly hungry. The two men were still in the room with me and still had smoke bellowing from their mouths.

Goodness knows how long I was there but night had turned to day and my hunger and sleeping continued. A high pitched screaming noise woke me which sounded awful, only for me to realise once I had fully woke that the noise was coming from me. I was so unhappy and scared and my terror was haunting me in my sleep too.

I whimpered and started my next plan of attack making eye contact with the two men, pleading for them to take me home. One of them looked at me and then threw me some food.

Even though I was rigid with anxiety I managed to eat this and the rest of the food I had thrown at me. My stomach was full and bloated but the food kept coming and I had no control over my appetite and just kept on eating and eating.

We lost Ozzie after leaving the tapas bar when she ran away from us whilst walking home. She ignored our calls for her to return and we were frantic with worry and fearing the worst that she had been hit by a car and was lying injured somewhere.

Paul unlocked the bikes and he searched for hours on end whilst I waited with Roo at Teddy in case she found her way back. Paul returned exhausted after searching the streets, beaches, harbour and any of the cafes and bars that were still open. She was nowhere to be seen but we rationalised our thoughts and presumed she would return to the site as she was familiar with the area after being here for so long.

As morning broke Paul continued to search the area on his bike which allowed him to cover more of the area in a quicker time whilst I again stayed at the site and kept imagining seeing her race through the gates. She never did and by this time Roo was also showing concern and pacing backwards and forwards to the gate of the site, clearly waiting for her to come back. The guilt kicked in for us as we shouldn't have let her off the lead the previous night and then we went through the what ifs and buts and drove ourselves mad with worry of where on earth she was.

It had been eighteen hours since she went missing and we had literally scoured the full town and all of its nooks and crannies. Our last hope was at the police station where we called in and asked if any stray dogs had been spotted.

The police station is in the main area of the town and I translated into Catalan using my iPhone to the officer on the other side of the desk. His looked hopeful and asked me if my dog was maroon? Maroon I questioned myself. I just said "si" and then two other officers appeared and I showed them a picture of Ozzie and they immediately confirmed that this was not the maroon dog they had in the pound.

I was so hopeful they had Ozzie and in sheer desperation wanted Ozzie to be a maroon coloured dog which isn't the most common colour for a dog. I broke down in tears here as I was now really concerned and didn't hold out much hope of seeing her again.

On our way back to Teddy we cycled past the tapas bar where we had been the previous night and thought as a last option we would call in again and ask if anyone had seen Ozzie.

The bar was just opening for the evening though already lots of people were sitting outside. As we approached the entrance the woman from behind the bar came running to greet us and yelling "pero, pero, senorita pero" at us. She took my hand and guided me to a seat and excitedly tried to get her words out. We exchange a misconstrued conversation mixed with a combination of Geordie, English, Spanish and Catalan dialect and the outcome was that she knew where Ozzie was.

She made a call on her mobile phone and told us to wait two minutes. I really didn't have a clue what was happening and the two minutes turned to ten by which time my worry had exceeded maximum level and I could feel my tears starting to well in my eyes again.

We watched as a silver car pulled up outside of the tapas bar and saw two very brightly coloured dressed guys getting out. Looking past them I could see Ozzie sitting in the back of their car, her head stooped low, and she looked exhausted. Seeing her made my heart leap from my chest and I ran and opened the door to get her out, in doing so being knocked out by the strong aroma of marijuana. I lifted her out and could feel her stomach was bloated, her freckles enlarged by the sheer amount of food that she must have consumed. One of the colourful guys commented that she likes to eat and had just consumed a pizza and a full tube of pringles!

They actually wanted to keep her and had already renamed her Dealer! We think they were happy with the reward money we gave them as they showed their appreciation by giving me a seashell that one of them had magically pulled from behind my ear! They were a right pair of characters, one dressed in a Halloween outfit with a pumpkin hat on his head whereas the other one had a full facial tattoo with piercings in every orifice. Lovely guys for who we are extremely thankful for rescuing our Ozzie and looking after her for the night.

Ozzie usually goes mad with excitement when we return after being away from her for thirty minutes so her lack of excitement at being missing for a full day and night made us realise that she was well and truly stoned. Her night away from us had resulted in her being taken in and rehomed by two very kind, yet obvious keen pot smoking young guys. They told us that they watched as she was nearly hit by a car and then wandered into the tapas bar where they were sitting. He told us that they took her home and she slept all of the night when she wasn't was crying to be let out.

Every day living with Ozzie is an adventure, she gets up to so much mischief and gets herself into some pickles with this being the first one she couldn't get herself out of. If only she could talk! Paul carried her back to Teddy as she was too weary and sleepy to walk.

Roo was ecstatic when we she saw here and she jumped up and down hysterically around her showering her with kisses. Ozzie climbed onto her favourite chair and slept for fourteen hours solid, her stomach still bloated from what she had eaten.

Oh thank goodness I got back home that day and reunited with my family and my anxiety has gone. I felt happy being home and do not want to go back with those smells and the smoke and those weird dreams. It is amazing how much I had eaten, yet was still hungry and my pizza and crisp diet didn't go down that well. Roo snuggled in by my side and I really had missed her and so wish I had never stopped off to eat the pizza left in the bush.

That's it, lesson learnt! Well until the next time that is.

CHAPTER SIXTEEN

SHARK ON A LEASH!

We decided to follow the sun during the winter months and our route took us down the east coast of Spain and into Andalucía where we found ourselves arriving just by chance at Almerimar. A beautiful place with a motorhome stop in the harbour and right next to the beach. It was nearing Christmas and the site had all of the trimmings. Electricity, Wi-Fi, showers and fresh water though at 14 euro a night it wasn't the cheapest place.

This was however a welcome refuge as our previous night in Agua Amarga had been a free spot near the beach and looked too good to be true. Which we later found out it was, as we were woken by villagers in the early hours, loudly animating that the tide was coming in, before they helped us to safety.

We were shocked to realise that whilst sleeping the sea had been creeping ever so slowly towards us and if it hadn't been for the very kind locals we could have been in trouble. Once safe, we chatted to the locals who explained that the Mediterranean Sea is largely non tidal, though any winds can influence the waters direction and flooding here is common. We subsequently left a review to this effect on camper contact advising caution though as I've since read that fifteen motorhomes were rescued from here, it looks like people are still willing to take a chance.

After our unexpected 5am wakeup call we arrived in Almerimar at the harbour early morning to find an abundance of sailing boats and a vibrant and happy environment. There were crowds of people laughing and enjoying breakfast at Mario's bar close by which became our local for the duration of our stay who do the most amazing selection of tapas which is all home cooked and absolutely delicious.

Each morning we would head out onto the beach and run to the end of the promenade towards Castillo de Guardias Viejas which was approximately a 10 kilometre round trip and this was our routine every day with or without the dogs, depending on how keen they were to leave Teddy or whether they wanted to stay in bed.

On this one occasion I noticed a dog lurking behind us as we all ran along and Ozzie in particular was becoming increasingly worried and kept stopping and looking back. We think it may have been a stray though I could see it still had a collar and lead attached to its neck so it could have escaped from its owner.

It looked unkempt and had a dull brown matted coat that was thick with dirt and scabs. As it got closer to us it smelt awful and its nails were so long they dragged along the pavement.

I kept looking back and checking on Ozzie and Roo and could see they had noticed it too and Ozzie in particular was aware of its presence getting closer and closer to her. On a few occasions I shooed it away to stop it from following us but it was persistent and kept reappearing as we ran.

I noticed the other dog that had been following us that day and it looked angry and it didn't smell too good either. Roo's eyes were dipped as even the thought of being involved with anything nasty such as a smelly dog makes her weak at the knees. Roo was safe and not in the firing line for my potential attack and ran off away from me meaning I had to deal with this myself.

This is our space, our promenade, our territory so there was no way I was allowing this dog to get near us but it was catching up with and running faster and getting closer.

It wouldn't go away and it started to frighten me so I ran close to Emma for safety but the dog just followed me, so close in fact that it went to sniff my bottom. I allowed this to happen and remained still, like a statue as I couldn't move. My legs were stuck to the ground. It was a female dog and she smelt the fear that I had for her and then my anxiety started and my body was shaking, she had an awful glint in her eye.

She moved from sniffing my bottom to sniffing at my nose and hesitantly I allowed her to do this, then she moved backwards away from me. Thank goodness she was leaving me alone. The relief was overwhelming and thought I was off the hook and free to run off and find Roo.

My heart was pounding and I wanted to move but my paws were stuck to the pavement, literally petrified of this awful bitch who was troubling me was lurking close.

Due to my inability to move I was frozen to the pavement with fear she approached me again and being an easy target I guess I made this easy for her. I turned my head so not to look at her but she wanted to see my eyes and turned to look at them. It was that moment that I felt the dead weight of her on my back as she spun me around with her teeth tightly gripped around my neck.

I wriggled to shake her off but she was so heavy and much larger than me I didn't have the strength to rid her. Then I felt the sudden stabbing pain around my throat which sent me into a panic, she was biting me, my cries and yelps echoed around me.

I tried desperately to get her off me and rolled onto my back but by now she had her teeth firmly in my back and rolling onto my back made her latch on and bite down even more. I heard a piercing, gut wrenching noise and realised it was coming from me as I cried in agony, pleading for her to stop. I felt her large canine teeth sinking again deeper into my back and the pain was so unbearable worse than any wasp sting.

She spun me around and as she took larger and deeper bites at me in a blur I saw Paul and Emma and they were shouting and screaming for it to get off me.

As I was being flung around mid-air I felt the comfort of Paul's arms as they cupped around my stomach and lifted me to safety and away from her. I was shaking and I buried my head to look away from the ghastly beast that has done this to me. I was in so much pain and lying in Paul's arms trying not to whimper too much as I didn't want to be a nuisance. The skin on my back felt raw and I could feel it stinging and the blood from this was running down my back and dripping onto the pavement below.

We immediately headed back to Teddy where Paul placed me on my favourite seat and I buried my head in my blanket. I sat and whimpered in fear that she would return again and hurt me again. Roo came and sniffed me and but I did not move to see her. I just wanted to be left alone. Plus I hadn't forgiven her for running away and leaving me. I could have done with Roo there but no she ran off in the opposite direction, I was disappointed with her as she never came to help me.

My back was sore and uncomfortable when I moved and it was stinging with pain. Paul gave me cuddles and I felt a little more at ease when he was there next to me. I liked these cuddles and I decided to play on this for a few extra days as I realised that this attention was giving me treats in the form of biscuits, hotdogs, cheese and of course my favourite, tuna fish.

Ozzie thankfully wasn't seriously hurt and made a quick recovery after being attacked by the other dog. She was however left with a rather large wound on her back and neck and after a vetinary examination she had a few stitches and an injection of antibiotics that the vet promised would make her feel a little better.

It was so awful to see Ozzie being thrown around by the other dog who was twice her size and it was attacking her so furiously it made it difficult to part them, in the fear it would turn on either of us. I had never seen such hatred in another dogs face and it was really upsetting for Ozzie and also for us. We saw the dog appear and at first it seemed friendly enough as it followed us and sniffed at Ozzie which she didn't seem to mind. Something seemed to trigger its behaviour though we were not sure what this was and once it had accomplished its attack on Ozzie ran off and way into a nearby housing estate.

Initially this attack made Ozzie wary of large dogs and if she sees one whilst out walking she will bark at them. This sounds and probably looks aggressive but is simply her way or warning them off. We work hard on this and spent a lot of time socialising her with other dogs when out and it didn't take long for her confidence and naughtiness to return.

Travelling in a motorhome through Europe means that we kept seeing familiar faces as everyone we got to meet tend to stick to the same routes and it was always a joy to see our Belgium friends Philippe and Hilda, also known as chicken and saucy. I have nicknamed Philippe 'chicken' as his surname is Chasseur and Hilda 'saucy' as her initials are HP. Thankfully they have a sense of humor and take it all in good fun. They are a super couple and we have shared many nights with them eating good foods and of course sampling Belgium beers and local Spanish wines.

Saturday the 6th of December was a bank holiday in Spain and the small harbour town of Almerimar was buzzing with an electric and vibrant atmosphere with most of the bars and restaurants crowed with locals and tourists alike.

Saucy and I joined in with the celebrations and went out that evening to a local bar to salsa dance and we found a perfect place that was playing traditional music with traditional dancers. We ate tapas, drank wine, learnt how to salsa and joined in with the locals singing Spanish karaoke though we sounded awful. The locals loved us and they encouraged us again and again to dance and sing with them and looking back think we were their entertainment for the night!

We danced nonstop all night and ended up at a local nightclub where there was a grand total of six people, two of these being the bar staff. Mid dance I glanced at my watch and indicated to Saucy that it was 4am and time to go home. We swayed back to our motorhomes and that's all I can remember! Into Teddy and out like a light.

The following day I had the world's worst hangover, goodness knows how much wine and sangria I had drank and I felt and looked ill. So ill in fact, that I seriously considered getting booked in at the local hospital for the day. Looking at Paul I noticed that he too looked a little disheveled.

He told me about his eventful night which I couldn't understand as I had left him relaxing in the motorhome watching TV as one of our local teams Blyth Spartans were playing football against Hartlepool and he had accessed the game using the Wi-Fi.

He explained what had happened when I went out, was that some of the electric points had switched off and there was a knock at the door. The harbour master asked if the electric was working and Paul confirmed that it was fine.

Paul sat back down and was so engrossed in the match that he ignored Roo staring at him from the passenger seat. After repeatedly telling her to lie down or go to sleep she came over and pestered him by licking him trying to get his attention. Roo was so persistent and eventually when the half time whistle came Paul moved towards the passenger seat to see what was wrong with her and realised that

Ozzie wasn't in her usual seat and a quick search of Teddy confirmed that she was missing, again!

Flash backs from Palamos came flooding back to him and he became concerned as to where she was and how she had escaped. He took Roo's lead and they both headed off out into the buzzing nightlife of Almerimar and searched the streets and alleyways for her. Not a sign of her anywhere saw Paul grow more and more worried, though he couldn't face calling me to raise the alarm as he didn't want to spoil my night.

After searching for a couple of hours he returned to the motorhome in the hope she had made her way back but there was still no sign of her so back out he went, this time on the bike with Roo left in Teddy and he again searched the streets, harbour, pubs, clubs and beachfront. This continued for most of the night and into the early morning until 3am when he found her fifty metres from Teddy sniffing around the bins looking for food as if she didn't have a care in the world.

He had a feeling of relief and then anger. He watched how she casually sniffed each area of the bin and then wandered to the next and then the next. She was in her own little world and despite being lost for almost six hours she was in no hurry to return.

Roo and I spent Christmas Day in the beautiful harbour town of Almerimar. We guessed that this was a big deal for Paul and Emma as our routine changed. We weren't rushed out in the morning for a run and we were allowed to sleep a little longer. I could hear them singing and chatting in the cabin above me so I knew they were awake and then when they eventually got up they opened a large bottle that made a very loud popping noise that made me jump.

Peeking from behind my blanket on the front seat I could see them both drinking what looked like fizzy water and I noticed at breakfast time I got an extra portion of biscuits.

There was definitely something going on as Roo and I got a parcel which was sealed with tape and I had to chew to get this off. A little ridiculous don't you think, having to work and do something just to see what was inside the parcel.

It took me so long to open the damn thing, it drove me insane. I could smell the food inside and I clawed at the paper in a desperate attempt to free it and eventually I uncovered a small beef flavoured bone! Really, was it worth the effort?

Roo on the other paw was patient and took her time trying to neatly prise open the paper though she struggled to break into the wrapping. Of course I helped as I now knew how to do this in a quicker way. I scratched at the paper with my claw which made it tear easily and found another beef flavoured bone shaped biscuit that was clearly for me. Obviously Roo wasn't too happy about this but I guessed it was payback for leaving me when I was attacked.

The dread of humiliation struck again as Emma reached for the all too familiar bag that contains the most horrendous garlands. She occasionally puts these awful flowers around our necks on special occasions like when it's our birthday and I am aware that they make us look ridiculous.

She attached the flowers to Roo and I and we all headed out and arrived at a noisy bar full of people wearing ridiculous hats, drinking the fizzy water though I noticed the smell of food was delicious. There was lots of food going back and forward and I had already spotted the crumbs under the table next to us. I strained to reach these but got pulled back and I strained again and was pulled back. I did this again and again and my determination proved a success as I managed to get an extra few inches of slack on my lead and reached the crumbs. They weren't the best of crumbs but were still worth the effort.

Of course, as always, the attention was all on Roo and a small crowd had appeared and surrounded her and she loved being the centre of attention. One lady in particular was literally taking her love for Roo too far as she sat on the floor next to her and smothered her with cuddles and kisses. Roo lapped up the attention and gave kisses to everyone who noticed her. This *was a great distraction for me as I got lucky as my lead slackened again ever so slightly which allowed me to dart out and grab more food just left on the floor.*

I noticed everyone was drinking wine and also the fizzy water that Paul and Emma had that morning and I noticed this made them speak louder and some people also started to sing. We ended up there for most of the day and as the day went on the louder these people became. As treats for staying there all day I had some tasty food, though the beef and roasted potatoes were my favourite. I left the sprouts as they give me terrible flatulence.

Paul and I had a great Christmas dinner in a small bar in Almerimar called the Stumble Inn which I think is such a great name for a bar. Ozzie and Roo were great fun all day and Roo being the centre of attention meant enjoyed every minute of it, being cuddled and fussed over by the other customers there whilst Ozzie was on a mission to clear every single scrap of food left on the floor.

We shared a table with a lovely couple who had just bought a boat and had it in the harbour there. We talked about their plans to refurbish it over a year or two and set sail in the future to explore the world. Meeting people like this was inspiring and although we thought we were doing something amazing travelling Europe in our motorhome it's people like this who really motivate us.

Throughout the day people came and went and just as the tables were getting cleared, Riley and Elayna came and sat with us. They were moored next to our table companions and were a young couple from Australia who were sailing around the world despite having no previous sailing experience.

Their boat was called La Vagabonde which Riley bought whilst on holiday in Italy. Having not sailed before this was a risky investment especially when you factor in a freak snowboarding accident that left him injured only a few months prior to this.

Speaking with them over a few beers turned into a great evening and we were really intrigued and motivated us to hear their stories and plans and gave us some momentum to keep going with our own adventures.

Their stories were amazing and they reeled off tale after tale about the beauty of the Greek islands and catching tuna fish on rods cast out on the back of the boat, reeling them in and cooking and eating these on the deck of the forty three foot boat. We listened to stories about watching the dolphins ride the waves beside them and also how Riley had taught himself to sail the boat in the first place.

The stories prompted me to briefly consider a future travelling chapter for us in a boat. This was quickly extinguished when Riley explained the logistics of living on a boat and crossing the Atlantic. They were an awesome couple and totally inspirational and we left that night feeling completely content which gave us reassurance that we were doing the right thing too.

Being away from home comforts, friends and family at this time of year can be tough and very emotional and sharing our Christmas day with these people really brought to the forefront, how worthwhile the trip was for Paul and I.

Another amazing couple that we met were out motorhome neighbours in Almerimar called, David and Barbara. We were amazed to discover that David was 89 years old and having sailed the Mediterranean for many years he still would be sailing if there were no problems with his sailing insurance. Seemingly once you hit a certain age all the fun stops. They found another way to travel and bought their motorhome which they drove from Bristol to Almerimar each year. Nothing stops them and this sort of fight and determination can be catching as they truly inspired us.

Their stories and life experiences were amazing. They told us of their time when they sailed to Portugal from the UK and the beautiful scenery and sunsets they saw. They were a team and worked well together, bouncing off each other and very close and you could see they had a real bond between them often finishing each other's sentences as they had that telepathy between them knowing what each other was thinking or about to say.

That Christmas night Paul and I looked back on how our lives had changed so much and all for the better. We'd had a fantastic day with people we had only just met. Travelling means different things to different people though for me it is all about meeting people from all walks of life, learning from them and being inspired to keep on going. Travelling opens up doors and it gives you courage and a craving to do more with your life. Hence the reason we set out on this journey in the first place.

My fear has always been to have regrets and to one day end up in no fit state to do anything. Stuck in a nursing home unable to move and wishing I had explored more, saw more and achieved more. I have a burning desire and drive to experience as much as I can before eventually being turned to dust, ending up in a jar on a mantelpiece somewhere gathering even more dust just like Sidney and Miffy are.

My priorities before travelling were very different to what they are now. In the UK my 'things to do' lists would grow and grow with pointless chores and shopping lists that allowed me to feel that I was filling each day and ensuring I was busy and that I actually had a purpose in my life.

These priorities now include making sure we have fun, stay safe and rebel against beige at all times. Lots of people have dreams and aspirations to do things in life whether it's swimming with dolphins, walking the Great Wall of China or even getting a dream job and most never accomplish these and they remain just a dream. We only get one chance at enjoying life and in those final hours do you really want to be reflecting back with regrets that you should have done more?

Anything is achievable and your dreams and wishes can come true if you start to take action to make them work. Forget about that voice of self-doubt, go forth seize the day. I dare you!

We had been in the port of Almerimar for over one month and could have stayed longer but know we had the rest of Europe calling us and the reviews we had heard about Portugal were all positive so we left with a heavy heart saying our farewells to the people we had spent some great times with though we knew we would one day return.

CHAPTER SEVENTEEN

ON THE MOVE AGAIN

It's not every day you wake up with a slow cooker in between your legs yet after leaving Almerimar this is what I found upon opening my eyes one morning. We had spent a few days slowly moving towards Portugal and enjoyed some great walks around Frigiliana. One of these was to the lost village of El Acebuchal. The village was deserted during Francos regime and only came back to life 20 years ago when a family renovated one house in the village, then another before opening a bar. A great walk and beautiful place if you are ever in the area.

The following evening we arrived at a beautiful camping spot near the small village of Olvera. This site was situated on the Vias Verdes cycle route. This translates as green ways and are made up of old railway tracks that stretched for miles and miles throughout Spain and Portugal. This particular stretch was lined by almond and olive groves and early morning Paul couldn't wait to get out and explore. He woke early so decided to leave me sleeping and get out with the dogs for a run, explore the area and to see the sun rise.

We sleep above in the drivers cabin and share this with the box for the kettle, a portable oven, a fishing net, yoga mat and the slow cooker, all of which need to be stored when in transit and brought out once we stop for the evening. Living in a motorhome has led to us collecting things along the way. Some are items that we need every day and some are things we dare not throw out, such as the box for the kettle, as when in transit everything gets put back in its place to prevent any breakages. We've learnt to adapt to living in such a cramped space but all hell breaks loose if something gets moved and not replaced as this throws chaos into the mix.

Later that evening we ventured out and wandered around the quiet village of Olvera with not a person to be seen, only the flashing lights of Feliz Navidad still hanging from the buildings, left over as a reminder from Christmas. It was a ghost town, but we still managed to sniff out the only tapas bar that was open and enjoyed a glass of red wine and a tapas of tinned tuna fish on toast. Not like the delicacies we'd been used to in Almerimar, hence Ozzie got mine.

Due to the lack of nightlife in the village we thought it would be best to drive to Seville for the New Year celebrations the following day. Surely a city would have fireworks and a party atmosphere.

Seville city centre was very pretty with beautiful architecture buildings amongst rows and rows of orange trees and but unfortunately there was not a party in sight nor an atmosphere that indicated it was New Year's Eve!

We spent the day traipsing around the streets of Seville, sightseeing and stopping off at local tapas bars and cafes and were surprised to notice that around 5pm the shops, restaurants, cafes and bars started closing up for the evening and literally within minutes the city fell quiet.

A Google search explained that the midnight celebrations in Seville were held in the central square and the tradition is to eat twelve grapes. One to be eaten on each chime of the church bell as it strikes midnight and seemingly this brings you good luck and wards off evil spirits.

After heading back to Teddy for our evening meal and a few hours relaxing we walked back to the square where locals were already congregated around the church. We immediately noticed that the locals around us were armed with special grapes in tins which were tiny, whereas the ones we had bought were supermarket grapes that were literally the size of plums. The chimes sounded at midnight and Paul and I forced the grapes in our mouths gagging on the juices and seeds. It proved an impossible task as our grapes were huge and way too big to eat on every chime. Paul however managed to eat eight grapes whereas I only managed four, so we decided that between us twelve were eaten and we were content that this kept to the traditions.

The final chime was still ringing in the air and we waited in the hope of some huge announcement, song, celebrations, anything, to happen but to our disappointment everyone started to walk away and headed for home. We were completely deflated and after overindulging on grapes we didn't feel too good either. We had no choice but to join the convoy and headed back towards Teddy who was parked on a site a twenty minute walk away.

It was then that the fireworks started. In the UK there are usually organised firework displays but not in Seville. People bring their own fireworks and light them, either on their balconies or in the street in the middle of crowds and we watched as people ran frantically to escape these, ourselves included. The noise from these was incredibly loud and this was only enhanced from the buildings around us, the noise echoing around us. You can imagine that having two dogs in tow wasn't an advisable thing to do.

New Year's Eve 2014 turned out to be ridiculous and the opposite of a normal relaxing night in Teddy. Roo and I had been woken from our sleep and taken out in the cold to walk for miles in the dark without any explanation. It was cold, I mean really cold and I was pleased that Paul had put my jacket on to help me keep me warm. He is thoughtful like that, though he hadn't explained where we were going and I couldn't understand where they were taking us at this hour. It was our bedtime and very late and all I wanted to do was to stay in and sleep.

We walked all the way back to where we had been five hours earlier. Back in the city centre only this time it was filled with lots of other people and before long it started. The all too familiar feeling of being nudged, pushed and being stepped on. In no time my paws were black and blue from the clumsiness of some people who I think sometimes stand on my tootsies on purpose.

Out of nowhere some bells began to ring and Paul and Emma started stuffing their mouths with grapes, which was odd behaviour and was something I had never seen them do before. Then there was an almighty roar and together with the chiming of the bells this made me jump.

I used to be ok with loud noises and fireworks but nowadays I fear them and can only put this down to my age. The older I get, the more fears I tend to collect. An example of this is wind and thunder that I hate now but as a puppy this never bothered me.

What was bothering me, was the persistent banging and loud cracking sounds that continually filled the, air one after another after another. At first I tried to be tolerant but these bangs were getting way too close and one flew past, so close in fact that I felt the heat from this on my fur.

Quite predictably, these fireworks and loud bangs didn't bother Roo at all and she was still in a relaxed state as if nothing was happening around her. I on the other hand was a gibbering wreck! I wanted out, party, or lack of party over. I strained and strained on my lead to be free and although I wasn't set free we did start walking in the direction of Teddy. I was whimpering but these were ignored and I found I couldn't stop my body from shaking from my trembling paws right through to my tail.

When we eventually got home I curled up on my seat into a small ball and buried my head deep underneath my blanket. I could still hear the banging noise in the distance but being home made me feel safer.

So New Year's Eve for us was a flop. The festivities in the square in Seville didn't really happen and then Ozzie was frightened when the locals started to let fireworks off in the streets. The Health and Safety laws go out the window in Spain as far as fireworks are concerned. We saw people lighting these and throwing them from balconies and some were throwing them into crowds of people. It really was a relief to get back to the motorhome site and into the safety of Teddy.

Moving on the next day, 1st January 2015 we crossed the border into Portugal which was another new country for the dogs although Paul and I had previously visited the Algarve though not in a motorhome. This was the natural route to take from Seville and we had heard nothing but good things about this place.

Our initial impressions were that it was hot and far from the climate we were accustomed to at this time of year. Manta Rota was our first stop where we parked next to the beach for the measly sum of four euro per night. The beaches here stretched for miles and miles and the golden sand and pink clouds during sunset made this an idyllic setting to stop off.

Teddy stopped suddenly and Emma shouted our names to wake Roo and I. We had both been sound asleep as were used to the sound of the engine and its rocking motion sends us off into a deep sleep as soon as it moves.

I woke with a start and before I knew it I was standing on the beach and the sand was hot, in fact too hot for my delicate paws. Apart from a quick sniff around this morning I hadn't been for a walk today and I looked at Emma who was excited and she was right to be as this place was awesome and was well worth waking me up for. We slowly wandered along the beach next to the sea and she mentioned that soon it would be time for the sun to set. At this time of the day, the smells change and I got a glint in my eye, and that was the only cue Roo needed to give her the red light to make a run for it. We raced and raced off into the sand dunes which were filled with so

many different smells. My taste buds went wild as I sniffed and filled my
nasal passages with all of the delicious hidden treats of rabbit poo and stale
food that I found buried there.

I felt that this place was different, it was nice, it was warm and I liked
it. Roo and I had the freedom to run without being called back, which was
a bonus. When we got on the beach we came across some weird looking jelly
animals that Roo liked to pee on and there were hundreds of them, every
time we got close Emma would shout NO! leave it!

Paul and I immediately felt at home here in Portugal. The beach
was clean and quiet but we had to be careful as there were hundreds
of jelly fish dotted all along the shoreline. They had been washed
up onto the beach and some of them were huge. Roo got too close
to one and we think it might have stung her nose when she went
to investigate. Seeing so many jelly fish reminded us again of our
trip to Australia where warning signs were dotted along the beaches
making you aware that that they can sting you. Seemingly the advice
is, if you do get stung you can relieve the pain by having a wee on
it, the sting that is and not the jellyfish! I wasn't going to wee on
Roo's nose so a dab of antiseptic cream did the trick and brought
the swelling down after a few hours of her looking a little ridiculous
with an enlarged snout.

We found the beaches along the south coast of Portugal to
be clean, never ending and beautiful and this was enhanced by
the warm weather which for obvious reasons drew in the crowds.
Thousands of motorhomes from all over the world descend here for
winter. The Scandinavians seemed to favour the warm climate and
on reflection must have found the temperature and prices a world
away from what they are accustomed to.

Before leaving the site in Manta Rota we drove to the waste
point, turned the engine off and emptied our grey water. We then
tried to leave, I say tried as once again we broke down and Teddy

wasn't going anywhere! A few checks later we couldn't believe we had done it again and had ran out of diesel! Once was bad enough but twice. We obviously hadn't learnt our lesson from Italy, though whilst last time we played a game of bluff with the warning light, to my recollection it hadn't come on this time.

Luckily an English guy parked up nearby came to the rescue and drove to the local garage on his scooter to get us some fuel and as this was quite a distance away it would have taken us ages to walk so we were very thankful for his kindness. We weren't the most popular people on the site that morning with Teddy being stuck on the dumping area and fresh water fill and unable to move meant other motorhomers had to wait until we got fuel to allow us to move.

We donated yet another bottle of wine as a thank you to the very kind gentleman who had sourced the fuel for us and soon after hit the road and headed for Centieira.

We had the coordinates programmed into Connie for our next stop in Centieira and felt confident of getting there as we had read it was well sign posted and straight off the main motorway. Our confidence soon fell short when the road came to an abrupt end and turned into a dirt track, through olive groves and deserted old barns. We continued on in the hope of finding the motorhome stop but soon realised we were getting more and more lost.

By this time we had climbed quite considerably as the views of the motorway we had left some time ago was a distant blur. We had also driven onto what was now at best, a walking track piled high with obstructions of loose stones, rocks and fences that Teddy had to manoeuvre around. A group of walkers watched us with open mouths in astonishment, and as we drove past them. They must have been wondering how on earth we had managed to get there when driving such a large vehicle. It was time to stop putting all of our trust in Connie and begin map reading again as we had been blindly following her on a few occasions. Even though we had these mishaps we had continued to trust her and believed her to be right, for instance, even when she kindly guided us onto a military practice airfield in Belgium.

Back in the hills behind Albufeira we were pretty much stranded after reaching a sheer drop that prevented us from going on any further, though Connie was still persistent in her commands for us to keep going.

Miraculously Paul managed to turn Teddy around in what turned out to be a forty five point turn to get us facing in the opposite direction to start our descent. After much shouting and falling out with Connie we eventually arrived at the aire where we were greeted by a lovely guy called Pedro who gave us a warm smile and invited us in to his home.

The aire is based in the grounds surrounding his house and allowed motorhomers like ourselves to stay and at only 8 euro per night with all facilities included it was a bargain. On our arrival the site was full but thankfully Pedro managed to squeeze us in and once settled we felt very much at home.

Pedro gave us a full introduction, including a video presentation, which we had never had before, he was so friendly and made us feel very welcome. Being keen to explore the area the maps of walks of the area were useful and we picked out a nearby castle that was a decent distance for us to head out for a run there.

The free range eggs, and honesty bar appealed to Paul and the free cake offered as part of the initiation appealed to me. Pedro invited us to help ourselves to the three cakes sitting on his coffee table and as you can imagine I certainly did and suspect he probably regretted the open invite and I wonder if this offer is still made to new arrivals.

Other things on offer here included a car for guests to use, weekly BBQ, themed nights and a regular trip to a market and supermarket.

Trainers on and leads for dogs we headed out towards the castle in the hills and tracks surroundings Pedros but unfortunately we forgot the map. The surrounding area was beautiful and the scenery was amazing. We found a track that took us to the castle ruin, through a water mill and a ford that had small stepping stones to get across. Simple enough for us though more challenging for Ozzie and Roo. Nobody was about at all, it was quiet and it started to get dark and we were convinced we were walking in the right direction but in fact we were lost and this time we couldn't blame it on Connie.

A voice in the distance broke the silence and we could hear someone shouting the word. "fanny, fanny, fanny". This continued and was getting louder and louder. The sun had well and truly disappeared for the day and it was dark, our only light being from the moon and our mobile phone. We noticed a small dog had started to follow us and Ozzie kept making sure it didn't pass us and attempted to chase it away. We guessed that this was fanny and although the shouting continued in the distance we kept on going as we couldn't see anyone.

Fanny was a timid little dog that looked sheepish with no confidence, her tail tucked in-between her legs and her head bowed low not wanting to look at us. Fanny clearly didn't want to go home, she wanted to stay with us so, even though we were lost and didn't know where or which direction home was. She continued on our walk and ignored the calls from the person that must have been her owner.

After an age we were relieved to see the lights in the distance of Pedros and changed course and headed in that direction. Fanny followed us all of the way ignoring our commands to go away and leave us, even Ozzie warned her off on more than one occasion. Once we got back to the site she sat at the front gates and I couldn't just leave her there, the look of disappointment on her face that we were leaving her filled me with worry on how she would get back to her home. I ran back to Teddy and returned to offer her some food but she didn't want it. Instead she turned away from us and ran off into the darkness of the night. She obviously didn't like the food we had and didn't want to waste her time hanging around for more.

As Pedros was full and we had been squeezed in we only stayed a couple of nights and headed back down towards the coast as we were all missing the beach life and Roo was missing the sea. Another reason for leaving was that we had booked Teddy into a local motorhome garage to repair a few essentials such as the door not opening and fridge only working sporadically.

We said our goodbyes and left, looking for a place to stop for the night by the beach. Our favourite place in Portugal was found purely by chance just as we were driving past a small village we noticed a camping aire and pulled in thinking we would stay for one night and ended up staying there for seven weeks.

The little piece of heaven we found was in a place called Falesia and was the Algarve Motorhome Park. We pulled in and found a spot near the reception as most of the spaces were taken. The beach was a three minute walk away through a path surrounded by pine trees and led to some of the best beaches I've seen. Turning left took you to Vilamoura and right took you to Albufeira. Both routes had the option of walking along the beach or atop magnificent cliff tops which were a colourful mix of red, orange and golden tones. We spent many a morning running along the beach to Vilamoura and back via the cliff tops which made the circular route a good seven mile round trip and the dogs loved it. The cliff tops were extremely high and the warning signs along the way were a constant reminder to take care and stay away from the edge.

Once again I got lost! Distracted by food I then tried to find Paul, Emma and Roo as they had vanished but they were nowhere to be seen. I was just sniffing at a tree and looked up and they were gone! I knew we were heading towards Albufeira so I ran in that direction and despite hearing myself yelping again there was no sign of them. From my stomach I could feel my anxiety flooding back and I had to focus on controlling this and telling myself to be calm. I stood on the cliff edge looking towards Albufeira and the beach and in the distance I could see Paul, Emma and Roo. They were already on the beach and must have dropped down there whilst I was searching for food.

With no steps or path leading down to the beach I was desperate and decided I needed to rejoin them before they disappeared and so I leapt out into the air and fell down from the cliff towards the beach, I tumbled through the air, and before I knew it I landed on the beach below a little dazed but gave myself a shake and ran off to catch them up.

Ozzie decided to try out a canine form of skydiving and just as we spotted her on top of the cliffs in the distance she took the decision to launch herself off them. We watched her fall from the cliff top, falling around 120ft and her body looked tiny as she fell. We were helpless standing on the beach as we saw her tiny body turn and somersault as she dropped and crashed into the rocks and then amazingly landed on four legs on the beach below. The dusty sand bellowing from behind her was reminiscent of Paul and I learning to ski many years earlier with the powder trailing in our wake. Ozzie being Ozzie, simply stood up, gave herself a shake and then miraculously ran to see us with only the odd glance back to see where she had just fallen. Her white legs were covered in the red sand from the rocks and her face and body hidden by the amount of sand stuck to her, but apart from that she was fine, no broken bones and on we continued with our walk.

I was quite impressed with my skydive and it admittedly felt awesome and I can recommend you try it. I was literally flying, like an airplane I often see in the sky. At first I fell it was scary but once I was in the air it felt great. Thankfully I didn't even get hurt, apart from a few scrapes on my paws and back legs. Roo looked like she got a fright when she saw me fall and for the remainder of the day she kept fussing over me and giving me kisses but I was fine.

Being in Falesia for as long meant we made lots of friends and held several get togethers and motorhome parties where we all crammed into Teddy. We did attempt a dance on the table which nowadays isn't as sturdy as it used to be. Our Belgium friends Chicken and Saucy arrived one morning with a present for me that I had wanted for ages. A pair of retro roller boots and these provided an excellent alternative exercise to running and I still get these out at least once a week or whenever I come across a flat path or promenade. I wish I could record the looks of amazement I got from the locals as I whizzed past them, sometimes whilst being pulled along by an exhausted looking Beagle but I do prefer this mode of transport as it gets you from A to B a lot more quicker than walking.

Paul and I were well known on the site for a variety of reasons. Running every day, being the youngest there, having two dogs, one of whom we were constantly searching for, and mainly for the way we shared a shower. The communal showers were 50 centimos and lasted for five minutes. Too long for one person, not quite long enough for two people. However 50 centimos per day for seven weeks adds up when you are on a budget so I would go in first and wash as fast as I could with Paul waiting outside. Two and a half minutes later this would be reversed. Me out, Paul in. Not recommended, especially with only one towel left between us, as by this point in the trip we had ran short of such luxuries. The shower area was incredibly short of space hence the reason one of us had to wait outside. There wasn't even enough room to hang our clothes without them getting wet so again these had to remain outside. We found out that this has drawbacks when two mornings running we came for a shower to find Paul's underpants hanging there from the previous day.

Whilst here we had our first guest as my dad visited from the UK and our requests for him to bring us a couple of towels made showering time a little more acceptable.

He is a great cook and the dishes he made us whilst there were delicious and was even more impressive considering we only have a two ring stove and a grill that gives slightly more heat than you would get from a candle. Factor in these cooking facilities, along with limited space, three people and two dogs and it was amazing we managed to eat so well.

Our time here came to an end in February when the pine trees leading to the beach started showing signs of nests containing the dangerous Pine Processionary Moth caterpillar. Fellow motorhomers had previously told us to be aware of these as they can be deadly for animals. The numbers of these increased over the space of two to three days and whilst none of the animals on the aire suffered any difficulties we didn't want to take the chance so we moved on.

We explored the rest of the Algarve which we found pleasant enough and excellent for wild camping though nowhere reached the heights of Falesia. From here Teddy took us up the centre of Portugal where most towns we passed through were desolate. Youth unemployment is a major issue in Portugal and this was evident when driving through these towns devoid of youths who seemed to have escaped to larger cities in search of work.

The one exception to this was Peso De Regua, an affluent town situated on the Rio Douro and in the centre of a Port and Wine region. The aire was a car park by the river and cost us 3 euro per night and included electric, waste dump and fresh water, and we managed to pick up Wi-Fi from the local sporting club.

We had another flat tyre whilst here and unfortunately with no one around to help us this time we had to fend for ourselves. We noticed that the tyre had become quite soft on day one of arriving there and by day five it was flat. It was time to do something and as we were leaving the following day which was a Sunday so it was vital we got Teddy to the garage.

I had just made a large pot of lentil soup in the slow cooker and due to the implications living in a motorhome if we go somewhere then so does everything else we have and own. Including the soup. Not wanting to leave this I balanced the soup on my legs as Paul drove and he took care not to bump too much which was challenging driving only with three tyres working! I can still remember the noise and the look of astonishment on people's faces as we drove along the high street towards the garage on the far side. People were stepping out in front of us and waving their arms frantically telling us to stop. Sparks flying and by this time smoke bellowing from the tyre Teddy limped into the forecourt where he received not one but two new tyres. The other one had perished and desperately needed replacing. Reflecting back on the miles we had covered I guess Teddy has been good to us considering we don't take much care of him.

After the bill was paid for our new tyres we were ready to head off again and we had had a great time here with walks and runs along the river which recharged our batteries. From here we headed north east in the direction of Bilbao. From the reports we had read we expected two things, some form of life and rain, and we weren't disappointed on this account.

We stayed in the hostel car park at Bilbao who were happy to accommodate motorhomes and we also had the use of their facilities.

Where we parked offered a fantastic view of the city as the hostel was set high up on a hill near the Camino Santiago.

After a run around the city to familiarise ourselves with the layout we returned and visited the main attractions such as the Guggenheim museum. The design of the building was fantastic though Paul and I were both a little disappointed by the art inside. Thankfully a guest exhibition had just opened showcasing Niki de saint Phalle sculptures which more than made up for the other works of art.

The tapas in Bilbao was amazing with numerous alleys and small cafes tucked away all with their own unique tastes and styles. By chance during our visit Athletic Bilbao were playing Torino FC and although it was a sell out and no tickets were available, the atmosphere was great to be part of as the streets were full with hundreds of fans milling around for the event to start.

This is by far the best tapas of my travels here in Bilbao. We spent the whole day traipsing the streets and we went to lots of places and each time we stopped I got food. The quail egg and anchovy tart was a particular favourite and made up for the slow and boring walks around the city. Like I said earlier Emma likes me to try different foods and for future reference the octopus salad didn't stay down for long. Roo ended up with this after it disagreed with me and I vomited it up. Even though it rained every day and we got drenched to the skin with our fur wringing wet from the constant rain we all still had a great time. The stop offs at bars provided a chance to dry off and then as soon as we left a bar we got wet and then within minutes later arrived somewhere else where we dried off.

The camping aire being connected to the local hostel offered us a first as it included breakfast which saved us spending 60 minutes trying to turn bread into toast on our grill. You can use all of the facilities in the hostel and we found it to be spotlessly clean, friendly and they had a laundry which meant we could dry our clothes after getting soaked by the rain. Considering it rained solidly every day whilst we were there we used the laundry facility more than any other.

Leaving Bilbao our journey north continued, taking us up through France where we had a great time celebrating Paul's birthday in Epernay and wandering up and down the fantastically named Avenue de Champagne. From here we moved onto Château-Thierry which boasted a nice camping aire on the banks of the river and a McDonalds right next door. Perfect! We wanted to keep heading north but were undecided whether or not to go to Paris. We had both been before and loved it but weren't too sure what it would be like with dogs. After flipping a coin we decided to miss it out, decision made and Connie was programmed to take us towards Belgium.

We set off and no sooner had the words came out of my mouth that I was pleased we weren't going to Paris then my phone rattled and a text came through from our Belgian friends Saucy and Chicken. They were in Paris and this is how we ended up in this gorgeous city that Friday night. We were impressed to find the camping aire for motorhomes close to the city and the Longchamp race course. There was adequate space to exercise the dogs and we had a great couple of day's there walking and running and catching up with our motorhoming friends. This is the beauty of having a motorhome as you can go wherever you want when you want and plans can change all of the time.

Our route from Paris meandered northwards, into Belgium and then back to the UK for a few weeks for a family party and my friends Alli and Chris's wedding. This also gave us the chance to get Teddy fixed and through the MOT for our next trip. He was starting to fall to bits and was looking tired and in much need of a spruce up, oil and filter change and a good once over to get him back into shape to continue our trip to Scandinavia.

CHAPTER EIGHTEEN

FROM REMOTE TO MADNESS

We had to go back to the UK and I only found this out as we visited the vet again and Roo and I had to have an injection. As there was nothing else wrong with us we were literally in and out in a matter of minutes and as the vet spoke Flemish I didn't have a clue what he was saying to me and conversation was limited. Emma had our passports with her and used her telephone for translation but as I say he was quick to administer our treatment and that's the main thing for me. As you know I don't like hanging around these places especially after the many hours I've spent in these places with Miffy.

The vet stamped our passports which confirmed we were now legally allowed to travel to the UK. After a night in Ypres we headed to Dunkirk and Paul drove Teddy onto the ferry and was directed into the parking space. Roo and I were used to the routine, whenever we were left we were given a treat and wrapped in our blankets and then Paul and Emma left us. It was only a short trip so we didn't mind it much and we always get a treat when they return, so have something to look forward to.

Arriving back in the UK after being away for so long was strange as we had developed a routine of freedom and flexibility but found having a motorhome in the UK was very inflexible. Driving from Dover to Newcastle was a real eye opener in particular the volume of traffic on the roads. Compared to the roads we had just left behind, where we were often the only vehicle in sight, the Dartford Crossing was bottle necked and was more like rush hour in Beijing. The other difference was that the manned booths were in the process of being removed and there were no visible signs that indicated how much or to whom we had to pay to make the crossing. Thankfully we spent that evening in Mow Cop with our friends Tony and Sandra who explained that we had until midnight the following day to make payment. The fine for not paying the £2.50 crossing was £70 and as we were very nearly caught out this wouldn't provide the best of starts for motorhomes or any vehicles visiting the UK.

There are numerous pub stops across the UK which we used as we slowly worked our way north to Newcastle. These vary in cost and facilities though all welcome motorhomes to stay in their car parks and most of them have electricity and water but usually have time limits to stay there.

Once we arrived in Newcastle we booked Teddy into our local garage and he surprisingly flew through the MOT, he had his bits and pieces fixed back together so there was no hanging around. After a few weeks catching up we said our farewells to friends and family and then we were off again back down the A1 with a ferry booked for our crossing. We were looking forward to the second part of our trip and had recharged our batteries back in Newcastle and made some minor improvements to Teddy. We made our crossing from Dover to Calais and drove straight to Ypres, as we know and like this area. There is a free camping spot close the river and town centre, and we pushed on so we could get to the Menin gate memorial that evening.

Arriving at Ypres it felt familiar to be back and after watching the 8pm memorial we walked to our local café with map in hand to plan our route. Scandinavia had been on our list of places to visit from day one but the problems with the water heater and our own lack of knowledge had prevented us from making it there. This time, we felt that ourselves and Teddy were better equipped and our plan was to be in northern Norway for summer solstice. A challenging yet achievable goal. We decided the ferry from Hirtshils at the top of Denmark to Kristiansand would be the best option for us to arrive in Norway to avoid the lengthy journey through Denmark and Sweden and we had previously visited Copenhagen which looked the main attraction on this route.

From Ypres we headed north stopping off at Amsterdam where we stayed for one night on an aire which was a 10 minute boat trip from the centre. The boats were free and frequent and whilst the site was basic I don't believe anyone visits Amsterdam to stay around their motorhome. As expected Amsterdam was literally swamped with bicycles, parked up in rows and rows or in multi storey bike parks. There were thousands of them and even walking the streets meant we had to keep our wits about us with constant bells ringing. Having to move out of their way was a full time job and memories of our previous time in Holland came flooding back.

This place seemed familiar but I was informed that I had never been here before in my life. It took a while to put my finger of the smell that lingered in the air until I remembered that it reminded me of when I went missing in Palamos. Walking through the streets I noticed how sleepy and wobbly some of the people looked and stopping off for a coffee and cake gave me the awful knot of anxiety in my stomach as I had the dreaded feeling on not being able to keep my eyes open. No matter how hard I resisted I couldn't keep them open and kept falling in and out of dreams. Weird dreams at that. Thankfully we didn't stay there for long and after a short ferry crossing I felt a little more refreshed and we were soon back in Teddy though I was strangely feeling ravenously hungry.

We continued heading north up through Germany and into Denmark where we made quick progress towards Hirtshils and the ferry port. We made one overnight stop in Denmark and used a vets on the German/Denmark border as Ozzie and Roo needed another health check to allow them access into Norway.

Boarding the ferry was easy enough and our allotted parking bay on the ferry was close to the bow which thankfully wasn't enclosed so I was happy knowing we could leave the windows open for the dogs to get some sea air. It was 6pm and it was a three hour crossing, the sea was as calm as a lake and the sun was still high in the sky and not a cloud to be seen for miles.

Paul and I made sure the dogs were secure and safe in Teddy and headed upstairs for the crossing armed with a flask of coffee and some smoked salmon sandwiches. After a few minutes of sailing we noticed that the sea was starting to look quite rough. The waves in the distance looked enormous and the ferry started being thrown around from side to side which only intensified as we continued our journey. The wine glasses behind the bar were clinking in their holders and other passengers were attempting to walk as I watched them tottering from one side to the other.

It felt as if we were horizontal for most of the crossing and we had to remain on the deck above as all motor vehicles are below and out of bounds during the journey.

We noticed the other passengers sitting around us had turned a pale shade of green and then the vomiting started which made us feel a little queasy. We couldn't sit any longer and attempted to wander around the lobby area, only to find that this was an almost impossible feat. The ferry was being rocked from side to side and just as we arrived the merchandise in the duty free department went crashing to the floor. Reaching the tills and exiting the duty free at the far end was one of the most difficult tasks I had ever undertaken.

Just like Ozzie would do in this situation I found a quiet place and meditated throughout the rest of the journey so not to be sick.

I was so worried for Ozzie and Roo and felt anxious just like Ozzie does and I wanted to see them and asked one of the ferry crew if this was possible. Despite, or possibly because of the circumstances I was told the rules aboard the ferry are that no one can go below deck once in motion and although I did consider ignoring this rule and unlocking the doors myself I knew this wasn't a good idea and slumped back into my seat. Our coffee and sandwiches remained untouched and the dogs couldn't believe their eyes when breakfast next day contained smoked salmon.

This was the worst crossing ever! As soon as the usual routine happened with blankets being put over us and Roo and I each got a treat, this awful moving sensation happened. The movement of the ferry was awful and it made me sick and Roo had a big poo on the floor which wasn't our usual routine. The waves crashed against us and Emma had left the window open to let some air in but this also let water in too. I was soaking wet and the rocking from the rough waters forced me off my seat. Reaching land could not have come sooner and with Norway in sight we both panted with relief.

The three hour journey felt like twenty four hours and we were both washed out when we eventually pulled into port. I raced to the see the dogs and poor Roo was upset about the mess she had made and Ozzie let out her frustration with an almighty howl that echoed across the decks.

I couldn't tell you how relieved I was to see the familiar faces of Paul and Emma when they opened the door of Teddy. I howled so loudly that I almost frightened myself with the high pitching scream that I let out. We got lots of cuddles and treats but I was too distressed I couldn't eat them only settling once we drove off and reached dry land but this still made me feel as though we were still moving which stayed with me for a few days after. This

*was an awful experience for all of us and one that I would not recommend
if you're a dog.*

Norway was an amazingly beautiful country and the scenery
whilst driving the never ending winding roads was breathtaking.
We made comments that some of the fjords and mountains didn't
look real and were more like a backdrop at a theatre. A friend said
to us that God made Norway and then gave up on the rest and I
would agree and say that God modelled heaven on Norway as it
is so beautiful. The waterfalls and turquoise waters, snowcapped
mountains were amazing and we never grew tired of this and at
times were gob smacked by its beauty.

There are very few people living in Norway. Just over 5 million
in fact, which we were told by a friendly assistant at the first tourist
information we visited. Looking back, the main people we spoke to
in the four weeks we spent in Norway were assistants from tourist
information offices. By chance we met two Newcastle United Fans.
One at, you guessed it, a tourist information office and another
at a petrol station where we stopped off for fuel. This is where
Ozzie carried out another ever so frequent disappearing act and
miraculously escaped from Teddy whilst Paul was filling with fuel
and without us noticing.

After filling Teddy with fuel and paying the attendant we went
to drive off and I glanced behind me and looked at the back seat
to check the dogs were ok when I realised Ozzie wasn't there, just
Roo staring at me with a worried looking face. The station was
close to the motorway and a few cars were zooming past so we were
obviously worried for her safety. We searched the area and couldn't
see her anywhere and as we were concerned the guy from the garage
helped us look for her too but there was no sign of her. We were
annoyed with her, yet frustrated, not knowing where she was and
how she got out. The rain started to fall and we got soaked to the

skin as we continued to run around the surrounding area looking for her.

Reluctantly we headed back to Teddy after searching for over an hour and we could see her standing at the door as still as a statue as if she had been frozen. Not moving nor making eye contact with us. Ignoring our calls and still standing like a statue she knew she had done wrong this time and judging from her bloated stomach she had been rummaging and eating something that was obviously far more interesting than being with us.

We continued our trip, thankfully with both dogs in tow and arrived at the Jostedalsbreen National Park where we stayed for a few days. This place was saturated in natural beauty and we enjoyed long walks and hiking in the hills. The dogs loved it although we didn't see much of them during our stay here as they were free to roam around wherever they wanted to. No one was around, no cars, no people, nothing but trees and mountains.

After a few days of a solitary lifestyle I became stir crazy and needed some interaction with people before I went mad. It was a weird feeling not knowing what was going on in the world outside of the national park, having not to seen anyone for days, no Wi-Fi, news or radio and no Facebook! To give you an indication of the remoteness we managed to speak to four people during our whole time spent in Norway. Excluding my step brother and family who we stayed with for a few days in Stavanger.

Before setting off for Norway we had read blogs about the cost of food and drink and so we planned like never before and arrived all equipped and well stocked up with plenty of food. Teddy was literally busting at the seams with food and drink we had brought from the UK. Whilst some foods were expensive we were delighted to see that fish, and in particular salmon was especially cheap and much cheaper than the UK, hence we ate this most evenings. As bottles and cans of beer are bulky we decided that our drink of choice in Norway would be red wine and chose boxes that transported easier and didn't take up as much room.

Our one and only night out in Norway was in a town called Kristiansund further up the west coast. We walked around choosing our bar carefully and decided on a small local bar that looked nice but ended up pretty much characterless with no atmosphere and only three other customers there. We were hesitant to order a drink as the price list was extortionate so ordered two of the cheapest beers which cost us £15 and trying to make them last for as long as possible reminded me of my student days. This establishment wasn't dog friendly and Ozzie and Roo didn't look very happy as they stared at us through the window though this did give us an excuse not to order another beer. It wasn't the best of experiences and felt like we were a million miles away from the social scene we are used to in Newcastle.

The main reason for going to Norway at this time of year was to be there for summer solstice on 20th of June. We made it up to the Storjord National park where we enjoyed brilliant sunshine twenty four hours a day. Hiking and running at midnight was amazing but played havoc with our body clock and we found ourselves resisting the urge to snooze through the day and then lay awake at night unable to sleep. We had to start to close the blinds in Teddy at night to block out the sun to trick our bodies that it was actually night time.

Whilst there we met Camilla who worked at the tourist information and also owns and runs the smallest hotel in Norway, The Storjord Hotel. Built in 1923 by her great grandparents the hotel closed in 1940 before reopening in 2009. She showed us around the five bedroomed establishment where they also live and work in the summer months and it was stunning and situated in a picture perfect spot surrounded by meadows where wild deer roam. I have always wanted some deer antlers and after Scotland I thought walking in Norway offered the best chance of finding some on the ground. Despite looking at the ground most of the time in search for some I hadn't seen any. Paul had mentioned this to Camilla whilst chatting at the tourist information and as a gift Camilla very kindly gave me a large pair of antlers from the surplus she had lying around the hotel. I love these and pride myself on the thought that not many motorhomes travel around with a set of antlers. Much more important than solar panels and a working TV. Obviously space is limited in Teddy to store these so now they live in the cabin where we sleep along with the rest of our clutter.

Continuing further north we visited numerous places on the way all with outstanding beauty but as we clocked up the miles we were aware of a noise that had developed that seemed to be coming from underneath Teddy. This noise became louder and louder and after stopping on numerous occasions to check we continued turning up the volume of the music to drown this out.

As the miles passed, the noise was deafening so much that we knew we had to do something. The noise worsened when Paul used the brakes and also when he turned left so we slowed down and rolled into a layby. The wheel jack came out for the first time in the journey and we found the bolts on the left front wheel were loose to the point you could turn them all with your hands. It was an easy job to tighten the bolts and make it safe for us to continue on our journey though goodness knows how they became loose and we knew that this could have been a lot worse if we hadn't stopped in time.

Our journey toward the Arctic Circle took us for endless miles and miles of picturesque vistas and changing weather. Often experiencing four seasons in a matter of minutes the ever changing landscape in this country really was unbelievable. One moment we would have windows open and brilliant sunshine and the next we would be driving through blizzards. There are so many motorhome friendly tunnels in Norway and we used to see how much the weather changed from entering to exiting a tunnel. Some of these tunnels stretched for miles and some even had roundabouts in them.

Along with the tunnels came ferries to travel from place to place and we found the transportation to get you across countless fjords very easy and reliable. Prices differ on the size of the vehicle and whilst a motorhome is considerably more expensive than a car we didn't find the costs too prohibitive.

Norway has many winding roads and you really have to keep your wits about you especially on the narrow and winding tracks. We had to be cautious on every bend and one occasion high up in the mountains miles from any town or village we encountered the local council maintaining the road and they had a large vehicle with them meaning we weren't sure if there was enough space on the road for the two us.

Paul thought there was enough room, so slowed down and tried to pass them but unfortunately he had misjudged and landed us in a ditch. We felt ourselves sinking further and further due to the weight and angle of Teddy and as a consequence lost the side panel and bumper that became dislodged as we got pulled out. Luckily for us the workers rescued us by fixing a winch onto the front of Teddy and easing us out from the ditch. This cost us yet another bottle of wine as a thank you, and within a matter of minutes we were on our way minus a bumper, panel and a wheel trim.

Dusting ourselves off we continued with our goal being to reach the Arctic Circle which had taken around 1600km to get there, the length of the journey since getting off the ferry and arriving in Norway so you can imagine we had endured a few long days of driving.

The snow on our ascent to the Arctic Circle started to appear which made the scenery even more dramatic. It was a monumental moment for us all to reach the circle and being there exceeded my expectations. Not seeing any motorhomes for days it was a surprise to see this place busy with tour buses, tourists and a few other motorhomers. Once there we noticed how the landscape changed from the beautiful mountains, waterfalls and lakes to flat baron grey land.

We all left Teddy and toured around the site and noticed the sun looked different and had formed into what we now know to be called a halo sun where the particles in the air react with the sun and create a huge halo around it. We were extremely lucky to see this and was one of our high moments for us on this trip. Lots of American tourists were there and noticing they hadn't spotted the halo I pointed this out to them and then the excitement rose with gasps of, "Oh my god, that is awesome". If I received a euro for every time I heard the word awesome I would have left a very wealthy woman.

Continuing on our route and saying farewell to the circle we were filled with excitement that we had made it to the Arctic Circle and we were on cloud nine and extremely pleased with our accomplishments.

We took the route from Norway into Sweden and then down into Stockholm missing out Finland as it was just too far to drive. We did consider doing this but the distance to get there meant it would take us at least another week and change our route considerably as we would need to exit through Estonia and Latvia. Finland and the other countries have been left for another trip. Another thing putting us off visiting Finland at this time was the thought of more isolation and we had heard that in the far north there were only mosquitos for company

Our arrival in Stockholm was on a Saturday afternoon and we were overjoyed to find the aire was a car park in the centre of town right next to the water. It was also free at weekends and we got the last available space.

Stockholm looked a vibrant and lively city which was a glorious welcome after being so isolated for weeks in Norway and the sight of people and the sound of laughter filled our hearts with excitement. It was also extremely hot, in fact it was bordering on suffocating.

Once we got parked up we took the dogs to a local park and it was no surprise to see them head straight to the water. Ozzie merely wetted her paws whilst Roo dived straight in and it was so nice to see her happy and free in the water as we sat and watched her perform her usually party trick which generated curious crowds around us.

I dragged Ozzie away from devouring the full contents of a waste bin next to us and encouraged her into the water but she wasn't interested in getting wet, she just wanted more food. It was a Saturday evening and there was a great atmosphere in the air. The pubs, restaurants and bars all around us were full of people, all beautiful, all blonde and all looking very stylish. I was frightened to look in the mirror to see what a month wild camping in Norway had done to me. We passed an outdoor bar and the noise of champagne corks popping filled the air and we wanted to join in. As Norway hadn't been as expensive as we had budgeted and as tonight's spot was free we joined the hordes of partygoers, with only Paul and I dressed in shorts, t-shirt, flip flops and dragging along one very wet dog!

I really liked the remoteness of Norway as Roo and I could run free without being called back and we weren't bothered by other people getting in

our way. Now in Stockholm and another new country for me I wanted to be out to explore and literally leapt out of the door as soon as Emma opened it. We headed to a park and Roo's tongue was practically dragging on the floor with sheer heat exhaustion, she nudged straight past me and dived into the water in front of us to cool down. I wet my paws though was more focused on a bin I had noticed which was bulging with kind donations that had been deposited from the locals. Half eaten doughnuts and french fries soon made their way to my stomach and I licked the ice cream that had dripped from the carton on the floor which made for an adequate dessert.

As expected on a Saturday, Stockholm was full of people which was a very rare sight for us after being in such a remote place for the past few weeks.

It was particular busy this weekend as we later found out it was a national holiday and where we had parked saw other cars coming and going next to us which at times made it a challenge to open our door to get in or out. Whilst cooking our evening meal we left all of our windows were open and a family of five pulled in and commented on how good it smelt and we exchanged a conversation through the window. Then within minutes of them leaving another car would pull in and the same conversation would follow and this was a great way to meet the locals. Thinking back I could have made some money from this frequent activity and should have sold freshly cooked bowls of pasta.

The people of Stockholm were so welcoming and in the evening we ventured out to a local café/bar situated right on the water. It was full of the most beautiful people, all immaculately dressed and we felt a little awkward at first with us wearing our standard attire of shorts and flips flops. Plus two dogs, one still full from emptying the bin earlier on and the other looking for a way to get back into the water.

Once we were served Ozzie and Roo strained on their leads to find us a seat where they decided they would jump on and they sat up perched high so they could see everyone. The owner didn't mind and they both became popular amongst the customers in particular Roo who got most of the attention as always poor Ozzie didn't get much of a look in.

We sat at the bar and I had a comfortable seat that allowed me to watch all of the passersby who regular patted me on the head and said hello. I also got some food bits which was nice but I knew that I still had the rest of the bin to eat that I was rudely dragged away from by Emma, so had this on my mind to get back to later.

Roo sat next to me and I could see her appeal as she looked beautiful and more attractive than me and as always got far more attention than me. I'm used to this by now but it is upsetting at times and I feel out of place here as everyone is beautiful. She posed for photographs and got hugs from the people walking past and just loved the attention.

My paws were aching and I wanted to rest, we walked for miles and miles, through streets and over cobbles which was boring. All I saw all day long was legs, legs and more legs coming towards me and on occasions some people walk into me on purpose! It took ages for us to walk through all of these people and Roo and I had to dart from one side to the other desperately trying not to get stood on and then all I saw was darkness.

The next morning we toured the city and were impressed by the accessibility and the location of our parking spot which made this literally a five minute walk to the centre. Back in a city presented doggy problems as Ozzie was knocked to the floor and dazed during our tour of Stockholm as a lady walked towards her carrying a very large ancient looking metal suitcase that Ozzie walked into. The lady obviously hadn't seen Ozzie and the weight of the case knocking into to her made an almighty noise that resulted in her falling to the ground in a daze.

We heard the noise when Ozzie and the suitcase met and then a loud yelp. Paul holding Ozzie's lead picked her from the floor, the woman only stopping briefly and then continued on her way literally dragging her case along with her, it looked extremely heavy and goodness knows what was in there.

The only thing I can remember is walking in the crowd and then seeing a suitcase and then I fell to the ground. I came around and was in Paul's arms and stars appeared in front of my eyes and then the pain in my head and my nose and then the swelling.

To avoid the crowds Paul took Ozzie to one side to make sure she was ok and comforted her as she looked afraid plus the swelling from her accident became apparent in the form of an enlarged nose and forehead. This only added to her distinguished looks and we felt so sorry for her that she had been in the wrong place at the wrong time again. She always bounces back and literally within minutes she was back to her usual annoying self and straining on her lead to the bins and scraps of food on the pavement.

Paul and I love how resilient Ozzie is and she never plays on her injuries nor craves love or attention from us, she is just an amazing Beagle who fills our days with a combination of love and dread of what on earth she going to get up to next.

Leaving Scandinavia our next destination was Germany and in particular the Romantic Strasse, as this is a route we had heard so much about and wanted to view the Neuschwanstein castle and the beautiful town of Fussen.

We were familiar with Germany from our previous visit so our route and trip through the Romantic Strasse worked like clockwork. We were however disappointed with the lack of life in the villages and towns on route. However the route did save the best till last for us being a town named Fussen which had everything we wanted. A great aire at 14 euro per night, good walking and running tracks and plenty of restaurants and cafes close by. There was also a heatwave whilst here with temperatures showing up to 40 degrees so spending most of our time submerged in the beautiful aqua green lakes there made this one of our top spots to visit.

We walked for miles here and one route took us to the Neuschwanstein Castle where King Ludwig II once frequented. The palace has appeared in several movies and was the inspiration for Disneyland's Sleeping Beauty Castle. It is a castle fit for a princess and I am still awaiting the keys for this. I live in hope. One particular day after many photograph opportunities we headed back to Teddy through the numerous tracks, parks and woodland. It was dusk and we could see deer in the fields grazing looking very content and happy in their own environment.

Ozzie was minding her own business and sniffing around, her usual nose to the floor, tail in the air stance. Stopping to take a photograph we watched as she inspected every blade of grass of the field with a look of intrigue on her face probably looking for food. It was then that we spotted the hare. It was a huge hare at that with thick grey fur and piercing beady eyes. It didn't seem to mind being exposed and so close to us and instantly made a bee line for Ozzie. Still content sniffing the grass the hare approached her from behind and gave her a tentative sniff which made her spin and turn in an instant coming face to face with the hare. It was like a comedy moment and I will never forget the look of confusion and surprise on Ozzies face.

I couldn't believe the cheek of that hare, I was in a world of my own until I felt its presence and I turned to the shock of seeing a wide eyed, long eared and downright rude herbivore. You can imagine what happened next? Well you're wrong, I didn't chase it. I stood in shock and wasn't quite sure what to do. Do I attack it? Or does it attack me? To be honest I think we were both confused. Luckily Roo broke the awkwardness between us and came sprinting towards me alerting the hare which made it run and wow could that hare run. Roo had no chance in catching it and was soon flagging and turning back to us within a matter of minutes.

After a few weeks enjoying the sites of Germany we added the Black Forest and The Mosel to our places still to visit and after a stop in Liechtenstein we entered Switzerland and visited friends in Zurich. Switzerland was expensive and thankfully our guests provided food and bus tickets and the visits to FIFA and the James Joyce grave were free to enter.

Our next stop turned out to be our final stop. The beautiful and picturesque town of Chamonix in France. This was a place where Paul and I have visited numerous times for skiing holidays and had always wanted to visit and explore in the summer months and arriving here made us realise how beautiful it is. Norway is beautiful, though Chamonix has similar beauty in a much more condensed area.

After a few nights in an aire here, I flew home to England for a brief visit. Whilst home I realised I couldn't face the prospect of another period of living within the confined spaces of Teddy. I had found my utopia and decided that Teddy should hang up his keys and enjoy a well-deserved rest for a few months.

Decision made Paul and I quickly found a dog friendly apartment to rent in Les Houches just outside Chamonix, somewhere we could kick back and enjoy some home comforts for a few months.

Travelling in a motorhome for over eighteen months had caught up with us all and meant we were in much need of luxuries such as endless hot running water, a flushing toilet, one you don't have to empty every day and just as importantly a comfortable bed that allows enough room for you to turn. Our only maps and navigation problems here are for walking and running purposes.

Being in Chamonix gave Paul the opportunity to be involved with local events and the UTMB (Ultra Trail du Mont Blanc) which is a series of running events that either start or finish in Chamonix and take in Italy and Switzerland.

Whilst here Paul was enjoying his running and goes out alone as he runs so far that we get exhausted trying to keep up with him. There is always an event on here for him to do either running or walking and the ski season is just around the corner. I love it here too, everyone smiles and I'm enjoying my life.

As I write, our days are filled with lots of running, walking and exploring in and around the Alps. Yes Ozzie still continues to get up to all sorts of mischief and no doubt she will be planning her next chance to escape from us. From her antics in Italy being washed out to sea, skydiving in Portugal and not to mention her kidnap in Palamos who knows what she will get up to next.

I hope you have enjoyed reading about our journey in a motorhome through Europe and I can say that over the last eighteen months my life has changed for the better though my behaviour has not changed. I am a well-travelled Beagle and have visited 19 countries, covered over 25,000 kilometres. I'm a happier Beagle and my anxiety is still there lurking deep in the depths of my body but it isn't as bad as it used to be. I have done something with my life and I still have more to do, more places to sniff out and explore with my family. I aim to pack as much as I can into my one life before I end up the same way as Miffy did, as grey dust in a box.

Miffy's box of dust has finally been laid to rest here in Chamonix which I am pleased with as she would have liked it here. It is my favourite place too. We walked up to a very high mountain so high in fact there was snow at the top when we reached the summit. Emma said a few words and as we stood together I understood what was happening and that we were going to release her. I watched as Paul carefully lifted the box, gave it a kiss then passed it to me for a lick too. Rest in peace Miffy, fly away and go and find your own resting place, I love you Miffy and one day we will be reunited but not just yet, I still have some more exploring to do.

Sitting on our small balcony, overlooking Mont Blanc, the sun is hot on my back I'm stretched out dipping in and out of snoozes, no anxieties, no knots in my stomach only a feeling of contentment and happiness, life is really good!

Make sure you enjoy yours too x

This is the route we have followed and if we have inspired you to try this or if you want to find out more then please contact us, we would love to hear from you:

France, Belgium, Holland, Germany, Poland, Slovakia, Austria, Slovenia, Croatia, Italy, San Marino, France, Spain, Portugal, Spain, France, Belgium, UK, France, Belgium, Holland, Germany, Denmark, Norway, Sweden, Denmark, Germany, Liechtenstein, Switzerland, France, Spain

You can contact us by using one of the following:

Email: goingforaburton@hotmail.com

: Ozwena Burton

: @BeagleBurton

Instagram: @beagleburton

Follow our blog: beagleburton.wordpress.com

ABOUT THE AUTHORS

Emma Burton travels Europe with her husband Paul and two dogs Ozwena and Uluru. She left the UK in 2014 and can be found exploring Europe in her motorhome.

She is constantly on the go, never sits still and is looking for a way to find three lives to fit everything into this one. Whilst always in a mad dash to see, do and experience everything, this trip has thankfully brought her more contentment.

Ozwena Burton is a naughty Beagle who gets up to all sorts of mischief. She is disobedient, greedy but at the same time, adorable in her own way. She enjoys eating whatever she can get her paws on and sleeping, and her life mostly revolves around food and getting lost.

#0049 - 050516 - C0 - 210/148/14 - PB - DID1444997